Turning Hearts to Christ

ENGAGING PEOPLE
IN A LIFETIME OF FAITH

LEISA ANSLINGER

TURNING
hearts
TO CHRIST

ENGAGING PEOPLE
in a LIFETIME *of* FAITH

TWENTY
THIRD 23rd
PUBLICATIONS
www.23rdpublications.com

TWENTY-THIRD PUBLICATIONS
A Division of Bayard
One Montauk Avenue, Suite 200
New London, CT 06320
(860) 437-3012 or (800) 321-0411
www.23rdpublications.com

Cover image: "Jesus Christ - Christus Statue" - flickr.com/photos/midiman (license-CC 2.0 attribution)

ISBN 978-1-58595-793-4
Library of Congress Control Number: 2010925812
Printed in the U.S.A.

ACKNOWLEDGMENTS

"I thank my God every time I remember you, constantly praying with joy in every one of my prayers for all of you, because of your sharing in the gospel from the first day until now."

■ Philippians 1:3–5

It is with a deeply grateful heart that I wish to acknowledge the prayerful reading, support, and companionship of so many as this book took shape and developed:

Father Bill Hanson, Bill Huebsch, and Father Jan Schmidt, critical readers and advisors extraordinaire;

Peg Sorrentino, the "Connect the Dots" ladies, Mary, and so many wonderful friends and colleagues at St. Margaret of York; St. Gerard Majella, Immaculate Heart of Mary, St. Clare, St. Antoninus, and parishes and dioceses who so willingly share their witness and experience so that others may be encouraged to learn and grow;

Cindy, Tish, Kathleen, and the wonderful people in New York; Rick, Patti, Scott, and the good folks in Seattle; Debbie, Debra, Don, Donna, who all show their love for Christ and the Church through dedicated service and love;

David Haas and all who are part of Music Ministry Alive; friends and colleagues who inspire selfless giving in ministry;

the community of St. John's Abbey, Collegeville, Minnesota;

Al Winseman, Jo Ann Miller, Jeremy Pietrocini, Laurel Kjersten, and all at the Gallup Organization whose work is the foundation of much of what is contained in this book;

The good people at Twenty-Third Publications, particularly Dan Connors, who edited this book with care;

and, of course, Steve, Mike, Carrie, and all our family and friends whose love gives me strength to continue to turn my heart to Christ, every moment of every day.

With gratitude on this feast of St. Benedict, 2010

CONTENTS

Does parish life really matter? Do people really need community anymore? We hear stories of "successful parishes," but aren't they just the special ones who happen to have the right combination of people for a time?

For what do you hope and pray when you think of your parish? For many years now I have asked that question in a variety of ways. The responses of pastoral leaders are strikingly similar:

- We hope that people will commit themselves to a real and lasting relationship with Jesus Christ that makes God a priority in their lives;

- We want them to come to Mass on Sunday, to fully participate in the celebration of the Eucharist and sacraments;

- We want our parishes to be filled with people who live their faith through acts of service, striving for justice, standing in solidarity with those most in need;

- We hope that people live their faith at home, in their neighborhood, city, and world;

- We wish that they would see the parish as an important part of their lives because in our hearts we know that those who are most deeply connected to our parishes are the people who live their faith most deeply;

- We want them to bring their family and friends with them, not just at Christmas and Easter or for special moments such as funerals and weddings, but throughout the year;

- We hope and pray that our parishes will be communities of people who know themselves to be members of Christ's body and who live as Christ's people in our world, drawing others to Christ or more deeply to Christ. In other words, we want our parishes to be places in which people naturally turn their hearts to Christ.

✐ Our Context for Turning Hearts to Christ ❧

In my conversations with pastoral leaders, I've noticed that many seem to have glimpses of life in their parishes that lead them to believe that all of this is possible and more, and yet they are so busy taking care of people and the "stuff" of parish life, they can barely think, let alone strategically plan for more effective and life-giving ministry.

When we name all that we hope and pray for, people immediately turn to the questions that lie most deeply within: Does any parish really experience that kind of life? How? Is that really possible? Is it realistic? Would we exhaust ourselves in trying to change things, only to find that nothing really changed? It isn't that the people and the stuff are not important; it is simply that developing effective pastoral practice demands change of us. But most of us are not sure where or how to begin, and we cannot imagine finding the time to start!

Still, we know that what many of us are currently doing is not working. We find ourselves exhausted by the pace and demands placed upon us (often it is we ourselves who demand so much—convinced that if we just try harder and longer at the same things, these things will somehow get better). Even with all our discussion and with consistent attempts to respond to the daily details and circumstances of our lives in our parishes, things don't get better. If we're honest with ourselves, things really do seem to be in a steady mode of decline for many of us: declining attendance at Mass, declining participation in parish functions, declining or static involvement in parish organizations, declining parish life. Even for those of us whose parishes do not seem to be in decline, we sense that something is lacking.

The data from social scientists bears out what our experience tells us: "While nearly one-in-three Americans (31%) were raised in the Catholic faith, today fewer than one-in-four (24%) describe themselves as Catholic. These losses would be even more pronounced were it not for the offsetting impact of immigration."[1] Similarly, we see data that detail the declining numbers of priests and vowed religious,[2] and we recognize that the current generation of young adults, often referred to as the Millennials, are less likely to affiliate with any religious denomination, even when compared to other generations when they were young adults.[3]

Studies by social scientists can do more than point out what is wrong in Catholic parish life, however. We may also learn to discover and develop more effective practices by applying social science research and tools. Those who have read about the impact of parishioner engagement[4] or who have attended a presentation on this topic recognize the hope and possibility of creating a more engaged parish, and we will draw on that research in what follows. Perhaps the most stunning finding in the engagement study is this: Empirical research points to the same outcomes of authentic community life as that which we see in the early communities of believers:

- Members *invite* others to the parish and so their parishes are growing;
- Members *give* of their financial resources and so their parishes experience financial stability;

- Members offer more time in *service*, and so ministry thrives in their parishes and beyond them, people are served, the gospel lives;
- Members are *thankful* people who are satisfied with their lives. They are happy people to be around, and their parishes are compelling as a result.

Does this sound familiar? That should not be surprising: "They devoted themselves to the apostles' teaching and fellowship, to the breaking of bread and the prayers. Awe came upon everyone, because many wonders and signs were being done by the apostles. All who believed were together and had all things in common; they would sell their possessions and goods and distribute the proceeds to all, as any had need. Day by day, as they spent much time together in the temple, they broke bread at home and ate their food with glad and generous hearts, praising God and having the goodwill of all the people. And day by day the Lord added to their number those who were being saved" (Acts 2:42–47).

Parishes that are growing in engagement experience the sort of life they only dared to imagine just a few years ago. Their life feels much like that which we see described in the Acts of the Apostles, and they become eager to share their experiences with others.[5] We will learn from these parishes as we explore the power of engaging people to turn other's hearts to Christ.

∾ Where Does This Lead Us? ∾

The first thing we may need to do is to reclaim the word "evangelization" so that when we speak of turning people's hearts to Christ we recognize the true nature of the process of evangelization and the important place of the community of faith in that process. "We know that the word 'evangelization' sometimes raises uncomfortable images for Catholics....Still, we use the word 'evangelization' because its root meaning is 'Gospel' (Good News) and because it calls us, even if it is uncomfortable, to live the faith of our baptism more openly and to share it more freely. Some might think of evangelization solely in terms of Jesus and our relationship with him. Yet our relationship with Jesus is found in our relationship with the community of Jesus— the Church. The way to Christ is through the community in which he lives."[6] So creating an environment in which people are engaged in their parish strengthens the potential that they will be drawn more deeply to Christ and that they will in turn invite others to our Lord.

Second, we should remind ourselves that each of us is called to a lifetime of faith, and our parishes must be places that foster ongoing conversion in Christ. But our efforts toward this goal must be realistic, not simply adding more to the already full lives of staff, key parishioner leaders, or the average parishioner. Rather, we can change and deepen the way we do the things we are already doing, building parishes that reach the mission for which they exist. "For most people, the parish…is the place where the Christian faith is first received, expressed, and nourished. It is where the Christian faith deepens and where the Christian community is formed. In the parish the members of the Christian community 'become aware of being the people of God.' Because of all this, it is the responsibility of the parish community and its leadership to ensure that the faith that it teaches, preaches, and celebrates is alive and that it is a true sign, for all who come in contact with it, that this truly is the living Body of Christ."[7]

Third, creating and sustaining parish life that is engaging and that leads people to a lifetime of faith will only happen when we take the time to discover what is already life-giving and effective; we must dream together to establish a common vision for ourselves as a community of faith; we can then discern the practices that are most likely to be appropriate for our people, which will lead us to design a plan in order to ensure that we will cooperate with the Holy Spirit to build a community that helps to turn people's hearts to Christ.[8]

✧ Who This Book Is For ✧

This is intended to help...

Pastors, as you lead your parishioners into a new level of belonging with each other;

Parish leadership teams, parishioner leaders, or pastoral staffs, as you uncover deeper connections among your existing and new parishioners;

Parish Pastoral Council members, as you yearn to build a path for your children and grandchildren to find their way back to church;

Faith Formation and Evangelization Committees or planning groups as you search for ways to inspire children and their parents with our stories of faith;

Stewardship Commission or Committee members, as you deepen heartfelt gratitude and widen generous giving;

Spiritual Life or Worship committees or guiding groups, as you strive to open the riches of our personal and communal prayer life;

Finance or Administration commission or committee members, as you create hope through fiscal responsibility and accountability;

Long Range Planning teams, as you scout out the path to your parish's future;

Anyone interested in contributing to the life of your parish, as you feel your heart turning to Christ.

The process this book supports will be most effective if you read it together, using the book as a journal, workbook, and planning tool. Each section includes questions for your personal reflection as well as prompts for discussion among your group(s). Set aside time to discuss each principle, and some additional time after you have studied all that is included in the pages that follow.

❧ How This Book Works ❧

Section One of this book is divided into seven chapters, each devoted to a principle for parish life. Each of these chapters ends with a process through which you may record your thoughts, experiences, and questions for later use in the final planning process. At the end of each chapter is a box that records primary themes or elements that will be carried forward into the strategies presented in Section Two. The seventh principle draws together the primary themes from the previous six. These are followed in **Section Two**, which pulls all of the principles together by offering a strategy to engage parishioners in a lifetime of faith through Seasonal Renewal. The seasonal renewal focus points are described, and examples of how the seasons can be developed and sustained are included. The book concludes with **Section Three**, which includes an Appreciative Planning process to shape your parish's life based on the principles and seasons, and consideration of qualitative and quantitative evaluation. **Three Postscripts** round out the book, with considerations for engaging people in the liturgy and engaging youth in a lifetime of faith. A final postscript includes web links for helpful resources, additional learning, and support.

✍ For Those Familiar with *Forming Generous Hearts* ✎

Those who read, discussed, and used *Forming Generous Hearts: Stewardship Planning for Lifelong Faith Formation*[9] will recognize some similarities in the design of *Turning Hearts to Christ*. This book's outline and rhythm will differ slightly, however, in that the principles more clearly flow from and are therefore stated at the end of each chapter. While both *Forming Generous Hearts* and *Turning Hearts to Christ* begin with the importance of belonging, this book's treatment of engagement reflects the theological understanding and pastoral practice that have developed in parishes throughout the U.S. and in Canada in the last five years. So even if you studied *Forming Generous Hearts*, do not skip section one! It is essential to all that follows. One additional marked difference between the two books is that this one develops one principal strategy for engaging people in a lifetime of faith, rather than reporting dozens of pastoral practices to build parish life. The feedback offered by many of you who read and used *Forming Generous Hearts* was that the examples were all wonderful, but they were quite overwhelming, and pastoral leaders everywhere have asked for simple strategies to form engaged parishioners, based in study and experience, supported by resources that have been developed specifically for this purpose. This is what has been done in *Turning Hearts to Christ*.

The **Principles for Parish Life** are born of pastoral leadership experience in parish ministry and in discussions with pastoral leaders in a variety of ministerial disciplines, through careful study of sacred Scripture, theology, Church documents, current research, and in conversation with friends and colleagues throughout the United States. The principles are all interrelated; together they provide direction for you as a pastoral leader as you guide your parish to engage people in a lifetime of faith.

Seasonal Renewal through many points of contact is a comprehensive strategy to lead adults and youth toward a living relationship with Christ that supports and builds upon the engagement of parishioners and has the Sunday Eucharist as its center. This section of the book is very practical in nature and, while it is not descriptive of a program with a beginning, middle, and end, it is rooted in successful parish practice and is supported by a growing body of resources that are used as examples. Where the *General* and *National Directories for Catechesis* and *Our Hearts Were Burning Within Us*, and books such as *Dreams and Visions* (Huebsch) and *Forming Generous Hearts* have all focused on the vision of lifelong catechesis toward a living relationship with Christ, this book along with *Great Expectations: A Pastoral Guide for Partnering with Parents* (Huebsch, with Anslinger) offer specific and realistic practices to support the vision we all so fervently desire.

The book concludes with an **Appreciative Process for Planning and Development**, along with considerations of qualitative and quantitative evaluation. The process is an adaptation of Appreciative Inquiry[10] and will help you to build on what is already contributing to positive, dynamic life within your parish. Through this process, you will be encouraged to *Discover* what is already engaging people in a lifetime of faith within your parish; *Dream* of a vision for the future together; *Discern* how you will build on what is already working to move toward your dream; and *Design* a plan to make your dream a reality. Make a commitment to develop and follow a long-term plan; that will ensure that your time and energy with this process will lead you and all in your parish to a lifetime of faith in which you turn people's hearts to Christ. Are you ready? Let's begin.

Section One

Principles for
Parish Life

CHAPTER ONE

Those Who Are a Part of Me

The next day John again was standing with two of his disciples, and as he watched Jesus walk by, he exclaimed, "Look, here is the Lamb of God!" The two disciples heard him say this, and they followed Jesus. When Jesus turned and saw them following, he said to them, "What are you looking for?" "Rabbi" (which translated means Teacher), "where are you staying?" He said to them, "Come and see." They came and saw where he was staying, and they remained with him that day.

■ John 1:35–39

"Jennifer told me you would be able to help," the woman on the phone said. "I've been away from the Church for many years, and find that as I'm aging, I miss the Mass more with every Sunday. Now my husband has been diagnosed with cancer, and I find myself aching for Communion. I can't shake this feeling that I need the Church now, not just because of the routine of chemo and appointments that's filling our lives; this is more about faith in the face of death and trying to find the meaning of life. Jennifer said you would understand. Do you?"

Like John the Baptizer, Jennifer knows Jesus and cannot stop herself from drawing others to our Lord. Sometimes her attention is poured out on a neighbor or friend in crisis, as the story of this phone call illustrates. Often, though, Jennifer simply shares her love of Christ and the importance of her parish in everyday conversation. She brings people to parish events who have never come to anything outside of Mass; she listens to the worries of friends whose children are the same age as hers and helps them find appropriate ministry connections; she touches people through her presence and her prayers in ways that are life-changing. Jennifer knows her parish is a big part of her life. In fact, she and her husband, Tim, turned down an exciting job offer in a different city because the parish was such a big part of their lives that they couldn't conceive of leaving. They tell others how belonging to their parish has affected them in ways they would never have expected: As we have already seen, they *invite* others to Christ through the parish; they actively *serve* in their parish and community; they *give* sacrificially of their financial resources; they have found *meaning and purpose* in their lives that they say they probably would never have found otherwise. Belonging in their parish makes a difference in Tim and Jennifer's lives and in the life of their family. Their belonging is touching the lives of countless others through the ways they naturally share their faith and hope in Christ.

Jennifer and Tim are among a growing number of Catholics whose engagement is changing the life of the Church and our ability to live as Christ's people.

✎ Becoming a True Community ✎

John turned the hearts of the two disciples to Christ, who as a result followed our Lord and remained with him. They in turn told their family and friends about Jesus, bringing them to belong with him as well. They were drawn together as Christ's very own, and their lives were forever changed as a result. Our parishes are meant to be communities who follow the example of John and the disciples. We are to turn people's hearts to Christ or more deeply to Christ, leading them to encounter and be encountered by our Lord. As members of Christ's body, we are meant to say to one another and to those who are not yet among us, "What are *you* looking for? Come and see."

In our age it seems many of our parishes are less real communities of people who are in communion with Christ and one another, and more often simply collections of individuals who live alone or in the nucleus of their family, with little or no grasp of the communal dimension of our lives in Christ, and with little or no appreciation for the true blessing of being with others. They cannot imagine life in which people's minds and hearts are opened to the depth and challenge of Jesus' way through the community of faith. Instead, our parishes are filled with people who come to Mass and leave (the *not engaged*) or those who do not regularly gather at the parish at all, and they seem to be constantly pulled down by those among them who are always negative, always fussing (the actively disengaged). The result is a dismaying flow of people away from a real relationship with Christ that is lived within the community of faith.[11] Most parishes would love instead to be filled with engaged parishioners like Jennifer and Tim!

It is more possible than you might imagine to become a parish filled with people like Tim and Jennifer. The research of social scientists is helping us to understand what it takes to bring people deeply into the community of faith and to help them live out their lives as disciples who remain in Christ. As more people become engaged, the whole community becomes more dynamic and compelling. We will combine what we have learned from Gallup Organization studies on parishioner engagement with examples and stories from real people in real parishes. And, in Section Two we will look at a simple strategy for helping people to become more engaged and committed to a lifetime of faith. In doing so, we will lead one another to plan to become a true community, the Body of Christ, which brings others to Christ through the community of faith.

The Importance of Belonging

Think for a moment about your own life and relationship with Christ and the community. What initially drew you to live your faith deeply? What encourages or challenges you to continue to do so? For most of us, a person invited us into something that helped us to feel connected to the parish, and that began to make a difference in our lives. The more connected we became, the more we felt we belonged; belonging within the parish helped us to open our minds and hearts to our Lord, so that we came to belong with him. And that makes all the difference—in our lives and in the lives of all we touch.

Discovering and Dreaming: Your Life

DISCOVER *How have you experienced belonging? What difference has this made in your life?*

DREAM *What would change in your life if you really felt rooted (or became more deeply rooted) in a community among others who have a deep sense of belonging to one another?*

Belonging makes a difference! Those who are deeply connected within their parishes (the researchers call that sense of belonging "engagement") are more than 3.5 times as likely to be spiritually committed as those who are not as engaged, and they live out that spiritual commitment in *inviting, serving, giving,* and *being satisfied with the circumstances of their lives.*[12] As parish leaders, we can learn to build engagement among parishioners. In the process our parishes will come alive with a true sense of faith in Jesus Christ, lived out in community.

The Impact of Engagement

- **Inviting** 64% of the engaged have invited someone to worship or a parish event in the last month, compared with only 5% of the actively disengaged;

- **Serving** The engaged more than double the time in service given by those who are not as engaged; on average 2.5 hours per week in community service;

- **Thanking** 61% of the engaged say they are "completely satisfied" with their lives, compared to 43% of the general population in the U.S. and 23% of the actively disengaged;

- **Giving** The engaged give 5% of their income annually to their parish (nearly 3 times that of those who either rarely come to Mass or those who are always negative)

By building and sustaining engagement in our parishes, we can become what Pope John Paul II described in his pastoral letter at the turn of the millennium:

> To make the Church the home and the school of communion: that is the great challenge facing us in the millennium which is now beginning, if we wish to be faithful to God's plan and respond to the world's deepest yearnings....
>
> A spirituality of communion also means an ability to think of our brothers and sisters in faith within *the profound unity of the Mystical Body*, and therefore as "those who are a part of me." This makes us able to share their joys and sufferings, to sense their desires and attend to their needs, to offer them deep and genuine friendship....
>
> Let us have no illusions: unless we follow this spiritual path, external structures of communion will serve very little purpose. They would become mechanisms without a soul, "masks" of communion rather than its means of expression and growth.[13]

Following the path of a spirituality of communion leads us to realize that *who we are together helps each of us, and those who are not yet a part of us, to be open to the grace and mystery of what we celebrate in our sacramental life, particularly the Eucharist, and to live accordingly*. Engaging people in a lifetime of faith through the community will lead us to the living faith of which we so passionately dreamt at the beginning of this book. As Pope John Paul II eloquently put it, however, this is not possible by focusing on external structures of communion, but rather happens by affecting the life within the community so that it expresses and grows in union with Christ and with one another.

✐ Getting Real ✐

But we are not talking here about an unattainable, pie-in-the-sky dream. Instead, we can learn from the experience of Catholic parish leaders who are building engagement, and we, too, can create an environment within our parish that helps real people to build real faith, become spiritually committed, and live out that commitment in profound ways.

We would do well to pay attention to a small detail in the gospel account from which we read at the beginning of this chapter. The narrative that follows the call of the disciples we have considered here is the story of the wedding feast at Cana. After Jesus performs the first of his many signs, we are told that "his disciples believed in him" (John 2:11). The disciples came to belong with Jesus and *then* came to believe in him. They developed a relationship with Christ and with one another, and belief followed. So it is with us in our day. While our parish practices often focus on helping people to acquire and articulate belief, the Gallup research indicates that something else must come first for many people: "The reality is that belonging is far more likely to lead to believing."[14] Like the disciples who first came to belief in Jesus as the Messiah, we too must walk with Christ in the company of others, and in so doing we will come to believe in him. We will grow in a spirituality of communion that leads us toward spiritual commitment. This leads us to state our first Principle for Parish Life:

> **Principle One: Become a community of belonging** in which people encounter and are encountered by Christ, through the Body of Christ.

Discovering and Dreaming: Your Parish's Life

DISCOVER   *In what ways does your parish foster a deep sense of belonging among its members? What practices or strategies are already in place to help people to be drawn to Christ through the Body of Christ?*

DREAM   *How might your parish grow as a community of people who see one another as "those who are a part of me?"*

Author's note: Having read the Introduction and Section One, it would be helpful for a small group to read *Growing an Engaged Church* together, perhaps using *Guiding Your Parish to Wider Engagement*, a resource I have developed that includes a Catholic study guide for *Growing an Engaged Church*. This small group's study and discussion will be extremely beneficial to the Appreciative Planning Process, and to all that will develop as a result. See the bibliography for more information.

Key Themes for Pastoral Practice and Planning

Build Belonging

Lead People to Live the Outcomes: Inviting, Thanking, Serving and Giving

(These themes are represented in the strategies found in Sections Two and Three)

CHAPTER TWO

"Real" People, "Real" Faith

The apostles gathered around Jesus, and told him all that they had done and taught. He said to them, "Come away to a deserted place all by yourselves and rest a while." For many were coming and going, and they had no leisure even to eat. And they went away in the boat to a deserted place by themselves. Now many saw them going and recognized them, and they hurried there on foot from all the towns and arrived ahead of them. As he went ashore, he saw a great crowd; and he had compassion for them, because they were like sheep without a shepherd; and he began to teach them many things.

■ Mark 6:30–34

Shannon sat down at the table with a glimmer in her eye and said to the catechetical leader, "I was just thinking last night about all that has changed in my life since that day I walked into your office. Do you remember? I was out of work, out of sorts, and really lonely. You didn't have a way to fix my job problem, but you did get me in touch with people who helped me search for one, and you helped me discover my talents. But that wasn't all. You encouraged me, introduced me to a few people, and helped me feel that I wouldn't be alone, no matter what. I remember looking at a quote that was on your bulletin board. It was from St. Elizabeth Ann Seton (I looked it up after I left your office). It said 'Be prepared to meet your grace in the daily circumstances of your life.' I thought to myself then, 'Grace? Wow, do I need that!' Now, I'm a real part of this community and I have the privilege of using my talents to help others who are confused and lonely. I know now something I didn't understand before—you weren't just saying the things that you said that day to get me out of the way. You really did believe that things would be all right, and you knew this community would stand with me no matter what. Talk about grace!"

Shannon is blessed to have found a parish that understands itself as a community of real people. Real people do not always fit into the tidy categories of our programs, and often real people come at times we do not expect, much like the people who came to Jesus just when he and the disciples were looking forward to some time away.

Real people are also much more gifted than most will recognize on their own. Each of us has been blessed with unique combinations of talents, experiences, knowledge, and skills. Discovering all of this helps us to accept ourselves and others as people who are created in God's image and love, intended to be, and to share, that love with others. Being part of a community that invites each person to discover her or his true self—and to be that special person within the parish and the world—is a gift beyond measure. Shannon's life is filled with joy and peace now, not only because she was able to find a job, but because she is a true part of a community of "real" people, living "real" faith.

Like many of the people whom Jesus taught, Shannon has learned more from her experience within the community than she did from the words that were spoken on that first day. She had come to the parish looking for more than she could name, and she found even more than that; she found a home, a place that values and reverences her as a child of God. Her community helps her to discover and develop her talents, so that she will recognize the true gift she is, and she is invited to offer herself to others as a living sign of Christ's presence.

Discovering and Dreaming: Your Life

DISCOVER   *Who in your life has helped you to recognize the special person you are? What difference has this made in your life?*

DREAM   *What would change in your life or the lives of others if your community more deeply valued and reverenced every person as a child of God?*

ᔐ In Relationship with Christ and One Another ᔐ

When people come to a parish for the first time, the first question they unconsciously ask is "What do I get?"[15] Many pastoral leaders first hear that and moan, saying aloud or silently thinking, "Yes, you might say it this way—'What's in it for me?'" But when we pause to reflect on our own experience and that of the others in our parishes, we realize that each of us comes to a new parish with a mix of hope and expectation. There really is more to it than "What's in it for me?" We might think about it in this way: Being a member of a genuine community means being part of a relationship, and every relationship carries with it expectations and hopes.

❧ A Few Words about Spiritual Needs ❧

The people who gathered around Jesus hoped he would give them something; Shannon hoped the parish would have answers or help for her. Shannon is not alone. 71% of former Catholics who have joined a Protestant denomination say their reason for leaving is that their spiritual needs were not met within Catholicism. Two-thirds of those who become unaffiliated say they just gradually drifted away from our faith, and now they have stopped believing what we believe.[16] The Gallup study bears this out. As people wonder "What do I get?" they are asking, "Will my spiritual needs be met?" and "What is expected of me here?" This also underlines the importance of every person sensing that he or she belongs, because in becoming rooted in the community of believers, we are more likely to acquire, accept, and live the beliefs of the community of believers, the Church. In Section Two we will examine a strategy that will help people to name their spiritual needs and have them met within the parish community.

On the other side of the equation, the parish has hopes and expectations for its members, too. As a community of faith we hope people will find a place with us that calls them to live as a disciple of our Lord in every part of their life. We expect that people will participate in Sunday Eucharist, get involved in an organization, offer time in service, and give of their financial resources. And, like any relationship, it is better to talk about these things than to assume that everyone knows what the others are thinking, since most of the time everyone doesn't know. It is important that we state our expectations clearly, not as a stream of coulds, shoulds, dos, or don'ts, but rather, something more like, "this is what we know to be important and hold each other to here in this community." The challenge, Pope Benedict says, is to find ways to help people rediscover the value of faith.[17]

Those of us who have a living relationship with Jesus know that there is no spiritual need that is not met in Christ. We understand that the celebration of the Eucharist is the fullest expression of God's love, poured out for us and for all. Still, many leave us because they feel their spiritual needs are not being met, and an even greater number remain on the edge of the parish for the same reason, attending Mass but not really connecting. What would happen in the lives of all those people, and the people they touch, if our parishes became communities that helped them to recognize in the celebration of the liturgy and in the community that surrounds them there, Christ, who is all they hope and long for, all they need now or will ever need?

"Charity is love received and given. It is 'grace' (*cháris*). Its source is the wellspring of the Father's love for the Son, in the Holy Spirit. Love comes down to us from the Son. It is creative love, through which we have our being; it is redemptive love, through which we are recreated. Love is revealed and made present by Christ (cf. Jn 13:1) and 'poured into our hearts through the Holy Spirit' (Rom 5:5). As the objects of God's love, men and women become subjects of charity, they are called to make themselves instruments of grace, so as to pour forth God's charity and to weave networks of charity."[18]

❧ Superabundance ❧

Like most parishes, Shannon's does not always get it right, but as a community they are learning to meet people as they are, to do everything possible to exhibit compassion, patience, and understanding, because they are learning to value every person as a unique and wonderful creation of our loving God. They try to take to heart the example of Jesus who set aside any obstacles to reaching out to the people who sought him, and they seek to draw out of each person the best of who that person is capable of being. They recognize that helping each person discover the gifts she or he has been given is greater than the simple recognition of gift. In the words of Pope Benedict XVI, "Gift by its nature goes beyond merit, its rule is that of superabundance. It takes first place in our souls as a sign of God's presence in us, a sign of what he expects from us."[19] They do all they can to echo the wisdom of the U.S. Bishops who tell us: "The Gospel speaks across time and space to each human being, each mind, each heart. It asks what we think about our lives, how we hope, whom we love, and what we live for. If faith is not transforming each heart and life, it is dead."[20]

Becoming a community that comprises and compels real people to real faith requires us to consider our pastoral practice not from the perspective of we who are already deeply connected. Rather, we must think about our pastoral practices as perceived and experienced by those who feel themselves to be, or who are in fact, on the outside. Practices that are found to be lacking must be revised, adapted, or discontinued. Initially, such examination might be painful, and the correction awkward. There are suggestions for beginning such an evaluative process in Section Three. Over time, those who experience the true desire of the community to welcome them as they are will give lavishly of themselves for others in return. These same people, on their way to engagement, bring others with them, more regularly attend Mass, embrace Church teaching when making moral decisions, and give of themselves and their resources to the parish. Shannon is a perfect example of this: When people realize that the community truly values them as a person, the community becomes of value to them, and they are drawn deeply to Jesus' way as a result.[21] There is no greater way to demonstrate this reverence for every person than to invite him or her to discover and offer his or her gifts with meaning.[22]

Let us go back to our gospel passage from Mark. In it we are told that the hour grew late and the disciples asked Jesus to send the crowds away to find some food. Instead, Jesus takes the little they had with them, five loaves and two fish. "He looked up to heaven, and blessed and broke the loaves, and gave them to his disciples to set before the people; and he divided the two fish among them all. And all ate and were filled; and they took up twelve baskets full of broken pieces and of the fish" (Mark 6:41–43). Jesus met the people as they were, inconvenient as it was; he reached out to them with compassion, and at the end of the day, he took the little that the disciples had and, blessing and breaking it, he made a feast! Surely Christ can do the same with and for us. Each of us is a person created in God's image, given particular gifts with which we are to serve in Jesus' name, for God's greater glory. By themselves, those gifts may seem small and meager, but when we recognize, develop, and offer them together, through the guidance of the Holy Spirit, we are able to accomplish "far more than all we can ask or imagine" (Ephesians 3:20). The whole is greater than the sum of the parts! Our parishes are to be the communities in which people are nourished in Christ, in which we ask God to bless and break us, to recognize our mission on behalf of Christ, and from which we are sent forth to fulfill that mission in the world. Real people, real faith, real life. This leads us to our Second Principle for Parish Life:

Principle Two: Become a community that meets people in the **real circumstances** of their lives and **reverences their experience and gifts,** as a sign of the true desire that all be introduced and drawn deeply into the living body of Christ.

Discovering and Dreaming: Your Parish's Life

DISCOVER *In what ways does your parish help people to know they are reverenced and valued? How does your parish help people to know themselves as gifted and talented people?*

What do you want to study further, reflect upon, or remember from this section?

DREAM *How might your parish grow as a community of people that asks "what we think about our lives, how we hope, whom we love, and what we live for?"*

Author's note: Hundreds of Catholic parishes are using the Living Your Strengths process to help parishioners discover, develop, and offer their God-given talents. The impact is remarkable on individuals and on the parish communities in which this process is being used. Many parishes are using "Guiding Your Parish to Live its Strengths" to help them strategically begin this process for lasting change and benefit. See the bibliography for more information.

Key Themes for Pastoral Practice and Planning
Meet People as They Are; Discover Gifts; Clarify Expectations; Meet Spiritual Needs

(These themes are represented in the strategies found in Sections Two and Three)

CHAPTER THREE

Inviting and Thanking

*"I love the Lord, because he has heard my voice
and supplications. Because he inclined his ear to
me, therefore I will call on him as long as I live.
The snares of death encompassed me; the pangs of
Sheol laid hold on me; Then I called on the name
of the Lord: 'O Lord, I pray, save my life!' Gracious
is the Lord, and righteous; our God is merciful.
The Lord protects the simple; when I was brought
low, he saved me. Return, O my soul, to your
rest, for the Lord has dealt bountifully with you.
I walk before the Lord in the land of the living."*

■ Psalm 116:1–7, 9

Father Bob has lived in the same parish for the last twenty-four years. His diocesan and teaching responsibilities have been many and varied, but in this parish, he has served, not as pastor, but as priest-in-residence, presiding at Sunday Mass, celebrating baptisms, weddings, and funerals, and taking part in the life of the parish as much as possible. Recently, Father Bob celebrated his fiftieth anniversary of ordination, and, naturally, his parish wanted to celebrate with him. That day visitors were greeted warmly, as they are every Sunday, because the parish recognizes that when we gather for Eucharist, each of us brings our lives, our very selves to the celebration. There was, however, a special recognition among the parishioners that day. They were celebrating Father Bob's anniversary. That day was to be an expression of their love, not only for Father Bob, but for one another, and a day of recognition of all that they are called to be and to do together.

It happened that the Psalm for the Sunday of Father Bob's anniversary celebration was Psalm 116 with its familiar refrain, "I will walk in the presence of God in the land of the living," and in the midst of his homily he said to the people of the parish, "I think it is very appropriate that we heard from Psalm 116 today, since it expresses what I feel about my life with you. With you, I have walked in the presence of God. We have shared so much together as a community, and it is good for us to gather together today in gratitude for all of that. This is not just a celebration of the anniversary of my ordination. This is a feast that we share together often, in which we gather all that is happening in our lives, bringing it to our Lord and to one another. Today, I am grateful for many years of priestly ministry, and I am grateful for you."

A community of people who reverence and value one another is a mirror and vessel of the immense love of God for us. "If one member suffers, all suffer together with it; if one member is honored, all rejoice together with it" (1 Cor 12:26). The parish that celebrated with Father Bob knows and lives this now and will continue to grow into this reality in the future.

Belonging to such a community calls us to be more than we would ever think possible, and often all that is needed is an invitation to be drawn toward meaningful participation. It does not take long for the relationship within the community to become of great value in the life of the individual; collectively, the community grows as a profoundly rich expression of Christ's saving love, poured out through the Holy Spirit.

Discovering and Dreaming: Your Life

DISCOVER　*Who first drew you into the life of your community? What has happened in your life as a result?*

DREAM　*What do you need in order to feel more deeply connected to others within your community?*

✐ Growing in Gratitude ✎

We saw in Chapter One how Jennifer's engagement causes her to invite others to Christ through the community. We have recognized, too, the connection between being rooted in the community and the willingness to invite others in the experience of the early Church in the Acts of the Apostles. Belonging leads to believing, and when we know that we belong, we are compelled to invite others to our Lord. This makes sense! When we feel our parish is such a part of our life that it is like family, we will naturally want those who matter to us to find this same sense of value, reverence, and belonging.

When people are engaged in their community, they are also dramatically more likely to be thankful people. "Sixty-one percent of those who are engaged in their congregations strongly agree with the statement 'I am completely satisfied with my life.' This does not mean they are happy all the time or that they have known no sorrow or hardship in their lives. It does indicate that because they are part of healthy congregations, they are better able to cope with life's vicissitudes. They have a sense of direction, stability, and peace that makes their lives ultimately more satisfying."[23] People who experience this sort of satisfaction in life express it in gratitude. Rooted in the love of Christ through the community of faith, they accept the crosses in their lives, share one another's joys and sorrows, and are grateful for the great mystery of God's love for us, which is shared most profoundly at the celebration of the Eucharist. They reflect the true thanksgiving that is at the heart of the word "Eucharist," and their minds and hearts are open in more genuine ways to the blessing, nourishment, and challenge that the Eucharist calls us to desire and to accept.

When we are in a community that values and reverences each person, we are able to find the grace to be open to transformation in Christ. We come to the Eucharist with open minds and

"We seek to form parishes that are vitally alive in faith. These communities will provide a parish climate and an array of activities and resources designed to help adults more fully understand and live their faith. We seek to form adults who actively cultivate a lively baptismal and eucharistic spirituality with a powerful sense of mission and apostolate. Nourished by word, sacrament, and communal life, they will witness and share the Gospel in their homes, neighborhoods, places of work, and centers of culture."[24]

hearts, ready to encounter and be encountered by our Lord. The liturgical feasts and seasons begin to shape the rhythm of our lives. Our Seasonal Renewal focus in Section Two offers a strategy for orienting people's lives through this seasonal rhythm. As we grow in gratitude, we find the grace to bring the whole of our lives to our prayer together: "And what do Christians bring to the Eucharistic celebration and join there with Jesus' offering? Their lives as Christian disciples; their personal vocations and the stewardship they have exercised regarding them; their individual contributions to the great work of restoring all things in Christ. Disciples give thanks to God for gifts received and strive to share them with others....More than that, the Eucharist is the sign and agent of that heavenly communion in which we shall together share, enjoying the fruits of stewardship 'freed of stain, burnished and transfigured' (Gaudium et Spes, no 39)."[25]

❧ Mediating the Lord's Call ❧

This takes us to the essence of the word "vocation" and to the role of the community in helping each member to recognize, embrace, and live his or her vocation. "Responding to any of these vocational callings is transformative and reflects a spiritual pursuit," Catherine Cronin Carotta and Michael Carotta tell us. "The vocational journey is a spiritual one because it is all about your life, but still not about a life that is all yours. It is about the desire to make the you that is a private individual meaningfully interface with the public. The difference between those embracing a vocational spirituality and those who do not is like the difference between those deciding to embark on a journey and those deciding to stay in the neighborhood. It is a spiritual journey that enables us to make meaning of the ordinary and sense the sacredness of it. Vocational spirituality becomes accustomed to mystery while never really becoming totally comfortable with it."[26] In a parish like Father Bob's, every person is surrounded and held up by others who walk as companions on this vocational journey. Father Bob lives his vocation to the priesthood within a community that reverences and values him as it does every person. Each person is expected to be himself or herself, and to live as he or she was created to be, no more no less. "People do not hear the Lord's call in isolation from one another. Other disciples help mediate their vocations to them, and they in turn are meant to mediate the Lord's call to others. Vocations are communicated, discerned, accepted, and lived out within a community of faith which is a community of disciples (cf. Pope John Paul II, *Redemptor Hominis*, no.21); its members try to help one another hear the Lord's voice and respond."[27]

Remember the psalm to which Father Bob referred at the beginning of this section? The psalm goes on to proclaim: "What shall I return to the Lord for all his bounty to me? I will lift up the cup of salvation and call on the name of the Lord, I will pay my vows to the Lord in the presence of all his people. O Lord, I am your servant…I will offer to you a thanksgiving sacrifice and call on the name of the Lord. I will pay my vows to the Lord in the presence of all his people, in the courts of the house of the Lord, in your midst, O Jerusalem. Praise the Lord!" (Psalm 116:12–14, 16–19). Being engaged leads us to be people who invite and are thankful, not as extraneous activities or duties, but flowing from the people we are, individually and, more importantly, together. We will be thankful people who respond generously with our very lives. We will turn our hearts to Christ, and we will walk in the presence of the Lord together. This leads us to our third Principle for Parish Life:

> **Principle Three:** Become a community of **grateful disciples who invite others** into God's abundant life in Christ.

Discovering and Dreaming: Your Parish's Life

DISCOVER *What in your life within your community draws you to invite others? For what in your life within your parish are you grateful?*

What do you want to study further, reflect upon, or remember from this section?

DREAM *How might your parish grow as a community of who naturally invite and are grateful?*

Key Themes for Pastoral Practice and Planning

Grow in Gratitude

Support One Another's Vocation

(These themes are represented in the strategies found in Sections Two and Three)

CHAPTER FOUR

Serving and Giving

"Do not store up for yourselves treasures on earth, where moth and rust consume and where thieves break in and steal; but store up for yourselves treasures in heaven, where neither moth nor rust consumes and where thieves do not break in and steal. For where your treasure is, there your heart will be also." ■ Matthew 6:19–21

When Sam first accepted an invitation to serve in his parish's outreach ministry, he was more than a little uneasy. He had never been to the area of his city where the group would be serving, let alone interact with so many people who are desperately poor. But something spoke to his heart when he heard the announcement at the end of Mass, and so right after Mass he found someone who could tell him how to get involved. While in the past he had placed a few dollars in the collection basket on Sunday, now he wanted to do something that might make a real contribution.

The place where the group was to go was a large warehouse-like building with a loading area to the side. Sam was assigned to the furniture section, and at 7 AM on a chilly autumn Saturday, Sam's life began to change. He helped people who had no worldly belongings load simple items of furniture into borrowed cars and vans. His arms grew tired from lifting, but he felt his spirit being moved, not with pity as he had expected, but with compassion; he found himself thinking, "These are people just like me. Each of them has a story, I'm sure; some have families, some are totally alone; surely my little part isn't much, but it is something." From that day on, serving at the distribution center became part of his life, and the more he did this, the more he found himself realizing how tremendously blessed he is, how he can surely share of himself, his time, his material possessions and money, and he grew in gratitude for life, love, and the many ways God has given him gifts to share with those who are in need.

As pastoral leaders consider those outcomes of engagement that we have mentioned previously, the one that many first react to, often with incredulity, is that those who have a deep sense of belonging within the parish give of their financial resources in a far greater measure—more than three times that of the actively disengaged people. The engaged also contribute more than double the number of hours given in service each week, compared to those who are actively disengaged. In today's world, many people remark that it is just as challenging, or perhaps even more so, to give of their time in service. Time is indeed a very precious resource for each of us.

We cannot conjecture beyond what the data suggest, but what the data suggest is compelling on its own, as is the lived experience of parishes that have increased engagement and have simultaneously increased financial giving and time offered in service to others. The research tells us that engagement leads to spiritual commitment, and spiritually committed people give more of their financial resources and offer more of their time in service than do not-engaged or actively disengaged members.

Forming Grateful, Generous People

When we form people as disciples and stewards, we help them to recognize their "need to give" as Sam spoke about in the story above. We will look more closely at stewardship in the next chapter, but it is important for us to remember here that when people come to be drawn deeply to communal life, they grow in their willingness to give of themselves freely and to a greater degree than they have previously given (or might ever have imagined themselves giving). Catechesis and pastoral practice can guide people to reflect on the depth of God's love for them and help them learn to respond to this great love with their lives. In fashioning practices of this sort, we follow the wisdom and guidance of the Church itself: "But this sense of responsibility does not come unless circumstances are such as to allow man to be conscious of his dignity and to rise to his destiny in the service of God and of men. For freedom is often crippled by extreme destitution just as it can wither in an ivory-tower isolation brought on by overindulgence in the good things of life. It can, however, be strengthened by accepting the inevitable constraints of social life, by undertaking the manifold demands of human fellowship, and by service to the community at large."[28]

Discovering and Dreaming: Your Life

DISCOVER *How do you recognize yourself living the outcomes of inviting, thanking, serving, and giving?*

DREAM *In what ways might you feel called to deepen your commitment to God and others?*

✒ Focus on Causes, and... ✒

One of the important considerations in all of what I present in this book is that in the past we have focused more on outcomes than on causes. Now, with our growing understanding of the impact of belonging, we know that we can positively impact the cause (belonging) of inviting, serving, giving, and thankfulness, and that doing so will result in an increase in the outcomes we so desire among our people. In the moments after Pentecost as the new community of the Church was being formed, it is doubtful that there was some major charitable giving campaign! It is far more likely that people were drawn into a relationship with our Lord through the witness and testimony of the disciples, and that this caused them to eat their food with "glad and generous hearts." In other words, they came to be spiritually committed and the outcomes developed as a response.

Having said this, there are three additional important considerations for our attention, which we will address in the practical strategies found in Sections Two and Three:

1. While it is crucial that we increase the sense of belonging (engagement) among our members, that is not to say that we cannot also provide opportunities for people to be formed in the fullness of what it means to be a disciple. Doing so will shape and give meaning to people's lives, enhance their willingness to participate, and open their minds and hearts to the depth of God's love for them and all that love calls them to be.

2. It is also very important to be attentive to an ongoing process of formation that will strategically and intentionally lead people to growth in their willingness to live the outcomes of engagement. Not only do people need to be reminded that disciples of our Lord live in particular ways (inviting, thanking, serving, and giving), we need to show them what this looks like, make acting as a disciple in these ways desirable, equip them, and give them opportunities to invite, thank, serve, and give when they are ready and willing.

3. The very sorts of things that already are part of parish life often contribute to the sense of belonging that is present. It is important to offer people the opportunity to share their experiences, to discover together all that is life-giving, and to identify what is creating the environment for engagement to take place. Then, plan to build on that in the future. In other words, discover together what you do best! Too many strategies for planning in the past have focused on what is wrong or missing rather than discovering what is right or working. That is why the planning process described in this book, an adaptation of Appreciative Inquiry, is used. The process builds on all that we know of what helps to build the sense of belonging among parishioners, engaging them in a lifetime of faith.

Let us return to the gospel passage with which we began this section. After being told that where our treasure is, there our heart will be, we hear, too, that we cannot serve both God and wealth. Following this, we are reminded that the birds of the air and the flowers in the fields are given all they need, and so will we be. "But if God so clothes the grass of the field, which is alive today and tomorrow is thrown into the oven, will he not much more clothe you—you of little faith? Therefore do not worry, saying 'What will we eat?' or 'What will we drink?' or 'What will we wear?' For it is the Gentiles who strive for all these things; and indeed your heavenly Father knows that you need all these things. But strive first for the kingdom of God and his righteousness, and all these things will be given to you as well" (Matthew 6:30–33). Being spiritually committed leads us to place our trust in God with this kind of whole-heartedness and whole-mindedness. This leads us to our fourth Principle for Parish Life:

> **Principle Four:** Become a community in which people are called **to give and to serve** with their whole hearts, minds, and lives, as an expression of Christ's invitation and call to give and to serve.

Discovering and Dreaming: Your Parish's Life

DISCOVER *What in your parish's life and practice helps people to realize they have a need to give?*

What do you want to study further, reflect upon, or remember from this section?

DREAM *How might your parish give more attention to the cause (belonging) that will lead people to be spiritually committed?*

Key Themes for Pastoral Practice and Planning

Form Grateful and Generous People

Focus on Causes

Build on What Works

(These themes are represented in the strategies found in Sections Two and Three)

CHAPTER FIVE

Stewardship and Evangelization

in plain English

"Listen! A sower went out to sow. And as he sowed, some seed fell on the path, and the birds came and ate it up. Other seed fell on rocky ground, where it did not have much soil, and it sprang up quickly, since it had no depth of soil. And when the sun rose, it was scorched; and since it had no root, it withered away. Other seed fell among thorns, and the thorns grew up and choked it, and it yielded no grain. Other seed fell into good soil and brought forth grain, growing up and increasing and yielding thirty and sixty and a hundredfold." And he said, "Let anyone with ears to hear listen!"

■ Mark 4:3–9

John's life has not always been this focused or purposeful, but for as long as he can remember, he has felt a call to live his life in a genuinely Christian manner. He says his grandmother instilled much of this living faith in him from his childhood and encouraged it during his adolescence and young adulthood. He just seems to realize that his relationship with Christ places certain expectations on his behavior and attitudes, and he would not be satisfied to live in any other way. Still, the parish has a big part in his life, and being part of the community draws him out of himself, sometimes affirming him, and at other times asking him to stretch a bit more in the ways he expresses his faith. His is a quiet discipleship, but anyone who comes to know him recognizes the power of one who gives unselfishly of his time, who shares sacrificially of his treasure, who willingly offers his talents for the sake of others, and who truly desires that everyone he meets will in the process meet Christ, who is the center of his life. John is a disciple of our Lord who lives as a steward and who turns people's hearts to Christ.

Until this point in this book, we have not dwelt on the topics of stewardship or evangelization, yet much of what we have considered is related to both. In fact, we have not really focused on our call to live as disciples either. But now, since we have prepared the soil with an understanding of the impact of the engaging community in the lives of people, it is time to turn to the ways in which people are drawn to Christ and live their relationship with our Lord as disciples and stewards. We might consider these the seeds that the Lord plants, bringing us to take the word of God into our hearts, to let that word dwell deeply within us, and to bring it to yield good fruit, an abundant harvest. Perhaps, a "plain English" exploration of these three fundamental concepts—discipleship, stewardship, and evangelization—is in order:

Discipleship: A disciple is one who learns the way of a master teacher. In the case of Christian disciples, the learning is to be lifelong, ever-growing, deepening, and transformative. This is not "learning" that can be memorized and stored away for some distant use (or not at all), but rather, it is the taking on of the very life of the Master, Jesus Christ. Disciples' hearts are turned to Christ over and over again, as we grow as good and faithful people. "Mature disciples make a conscious, firm decision, carried out in action, to be followers of Jesus Christ no matter the cost to themselves. Beginning in conversion, change of mind and heart, this commitment is expressed not in a single action, nor even in a number of actions over a period of time, but in an entire way of life. It means committing one's very self to the Lord."[29] Through our baptism, we are drawn into Christ's death and new life, and each moment of our lives is both a reflection of, and a carrying-out of, the mystery of God's love for humanity that is most exquisitely expressed in Jesus. But as the quote above reminds us, living as a disciple requires a conscious decision to live in a particular way, in the Way that is Christ's.

"In the lives of disciples, however, something else must come before the practice of stewardship. They need a flash of insight—a certain way of seeing—by which they view the world and their relationship to it in a fresh, new light. 'The world is charged with the grandeur of God,' Gerard Manley Hopkins exclaims; more than anything else, it may be this glimpse of the divine grandeur in all that is that sets people on the path of Christian stewardship."[30]

Discovering and Dreaming: Your Life

DISCOVER *In what ways do you know yourself to be a disciple of Jesus Christ? What does this call you to be or to do?*

DREAM *Who affirms and challenges you to live as a true disciple?*

Stewardship: Christian stewards are disciples who come to recognize that all we are and have and will be is truly God's. We come to understand ourselves as being entrusted with the care and nurture of these many blessings, to bring them to bear great fruit, and to give them back with increase. Reflection on the call to live as a good steward will lead us to grow in gratitude for all we have been given. This is not a passive thing; our real call is to cultivate our gifts, our very lives, and to give selflessly and generously in imitation of our lavishly loving God. "Jesus is the supreme teacher of Christian stewardship, as he is of every other aspect of Christian life; and in Jesus' teaching and life self-emptying is fundamental. Now, it might seem that self-emptying has little to do with stewardship, but in Jesus' case that is not so. His self-emptying is not sterile self-denial for its own sake; rather, in setting aside self, he is filled with the Father's will, and he is fulfilled in just this way: 'My food is to do the will of the one who sent me and to finish his work' (Jn 4:34)."[31] Growing as a steward puts all of life in a new perspective. We accept and willingly offer our lives to continue Christ's mission on earth. Gradually, we become more willing to let go of

> "Stewardship is an expression of discipleship, with the power to change how we understand and live out our lives."[32]

material things, of a need to control or hoard our time, of anything that has the potential to stand in the way of taking the gospel to heart. Stewardship becomes a joyful and guiding reality in our lives that calls us to share what we have with others, including the gift of our faith—which leads us to evangelization.

Evangelization: Evangelization is the process of drawing people to Christ or more deeply to Christ through the way we live, the words we speak, our actions and attitudes. As disciples, we know that life in Christ is compelling, and so it is natural for us to want to share our love of our Lord with others. That is the essence of evangelization. We, too, are called to be evangelized, to be open to the process of being drawn more deeply to Christ each day: "Evangelization, then, has both an inward and an outward direction. Inwardly it calls for our continued receiving of the Gospel of Jesus Christ, our on-going conversion both individually and as Church. It nurtures us, makes us grow, and renews us in holiness as God's people. Outwardly evangelization addresses those who have not heard the Gospel or who, having heard it, have stopped practicing their faith, and those who seek the fullness of faith."[33]

"Pope John Paul II, in his encyclical on missionary activity, summed up the three objectives of mission: to proclaim the Gospel to all people; to help bring about the reconversion of those who have received the Gospel but live it only nominally; and to deepen the Gospel in the lives of believers."[34]

✍ Evangelization and Stewardship: ❧ Expressions of Discipleship

With these "plain English" explorations of these three key concepts, we can see how interrelated they are, and how absolutely fundamental each is. One cannot call oneself a Christian without being a disciple, and it is impossible to live as a disciple without applying Jesus' life to our own. Disciples cannot ignore that everything is gift, because Jesus himself is the perfect model of stewardship; with his life and in his words, he taught us to take what we have, nurture it, and bring it to increase, and he told us that, in the end, we will be judged on the way in which we have done so in caring for others (cf. Matthew 25:14–46). Finally, disciples are people who are in love with our Lord. People who are in love share that love with others. Therefore, disciples evangelize and continue to be evangelized themselves, falling ever more in love with Christ each day. "Refracted through the prisms of countless individual vocations, this way of life embodies and expresses the one mission of Christ: to do God's will, to proclaim the Good News of salvation, to heal the afflicted, to care for one's sisters and brothers, to give life—life to the full—as Jesus did."[35]

So let us go back to the gospel passage with which we began this chapter. We are told that the seeds that fall on good soil hear the word and accept it and bear fruit, thirty and sixty and a hundredfold. And then Jesus says, "Is a lamp brought in to be put under the bushel basket, or under the bed, and not on the lampstand? For there is nothing hidden, except to be disclosed; nor is anything secret, except to come to light. Let anyone with ears to hear listen!" (Mark 4:21–23). Our lives are to bear the bright light of God's love, revealed to us in Christ, to the world through the presence and power of the Holy Spirit. We will most faithfully do this when, like John, we belong within a community that affirms and challenges, drawing us to inwardly perceive and grow in Christ's presence and to outwardly turn people's hearts to Christ. This brings us to our fifth Principle for Parish Life:

> **Principle Five:** Become a community that fosters **stewardship and evangelization as expressions of discipleship**, ways of living out our vocation as people of Christ.

Discovering and Dreaming: Your Parish's Life

DISCOVER *What in your parish's life and practice calls people to live as stewards and to evangelize?*

What do you want to study further, reflect upon, or remember from this section?

DREAM *How might your parish invite parishioners to take more deeply to heart the ongoing conversion that discipleship calls each of us to embrace?*

Key Themes for Pastoral Practice and Planning

Stewardship and Evangelization: Expressions of Discipleship

(These themes are represented in the strategies found in Sections Two and Three)

CHAPTER SIX

Small Is Big

faith formation in small groups is more than you expect

After these things Jesus showed himself again to the disciples by the Sea of Tiberias; and he showed himself in this way. Gathered there together were Simon Peter, Thomas called the Twin, Nathanael of Cana in Galilee, the sons of Zebedee, and two others of his disciples. Simon Peter said to them, "I am going fishing." They said to him, "We will go with you." They went out and got into the boat, but that night they caught nothing. Just after daybreak, Jesus stood on the beach; but the disciples did not know that it was Jesus. Jesus said to them, "Children, you have no fish, have you?" They answered him, "No." He said to them, "Cast the net to the right side of the boat, and you will find some." So they cast it, and now they were not able to haul it in because there were so many fish. That disciple whom Jesus loved said to Peter, "It is the Lord!" ◾ John 21:1–7

Ginny and Larry, Dee and Jack, and Pat and Dick have been together as a small church community for almost twenty years. They tease sometimes about knowing how one of the group members will answer a question before he or she speaks, but in the teasing it is easy to perceive the love they have for each other. They share their lives, trials and joys, and everything in between together. If one is hospitalized, the others care for some of the daily details that would otherwise be worrisome; if one is a new grandparent, the others participate in the baptismal celebration; they have come to know one another deeply, to share their faith, to grow in faith together. For them, being part of a small group has made a big difference in the ways in which they know Christ and live as Christian disciples.

The disciples who were on the beach with Jesus had become a very close small group. They had shared many moments together; they came to know one another and each other's families; they shared in learning; they served in Christ's name together; they experienced the depths of sorrow and heights of joy none could have dreamt possible. They stayed together through uncertainty and found the Lord in their midst, not only in moments such as this one on the beach but also in the days after the ascension, through the presence and guiding strength of the Holy Spirit.

✍ Small Is Big ✎

The only portion of the study on engagement in which the researchers, in essence, say "we are not sure which comes first and can only come to the conclusion that this is a both/and process" is when they report the impact on engagement of membership in a small group. What their data says is that those who are members of a small group score "significantly higher on every item of engagement—an average of 18 points higher!"[36] For some, feeling a deeper sense of belonging may lead us to become part of some small group, a Scripture study or small church group, a group of persons at a similar state of life, for example. For others, we find ourselves drawn to a small group, for instance, we join a renewal or retreat group, meet other young parents at baptism preparation, or we participate in the RCIA, and this connection with others helps us to feel that engagement that is so important to our becoming spiritually committed. Regardless of why or how we join, we cannot deny the importance of being part of a small group. Small is definitely big in this regard!

Discovering and Dreaming: Your Life

DISCOVER   *How has being a member of a small group impacted your life?*

DREAM   *Do you need to find a small group in which to belong, or to invite someone else to join a group to which you already belong?*

✎ In Friendship, We Encourage and Challenge ❧

Those of us who have been or are members of a small group understand the ways in which such participation can help us to develop
a deep sense of belonging. In a small group, there are people who
will notice if you're missing; you will be held accountable to follow
through on commitments you make; you will have other interested
persons who want to encourage your growth as a disciple of Jesus
Christ. In the words of the engagement survey, "In the last six months,
someone in my parish has talked to me about the progress of my spiritual growth."[37] When people are part of some small group, it is much
more likely that someone might say, "How was that retreat you were
going on last month?" or "You told me last week about that Bible
commentary you are reading and I am reading it now too. Maybe we
could talk about it sometime soon." In other words, when we belong
to a small group, it is easier for us to build relationships that draw us
more deeply into the community, and we are more likely to be held
accountable to follow through in ways that will lead to our spiritual
commitment.

"Many parishes include small Christian communities, which arise
because the faithful want to 'live the Church's life more intensely,
or from the desire and quest for a more human dimension such as
larger ecclesial communities can only offer with difficulty.' Small
Christian communities are important centers for the cultivation of
both Christian virtues and human values. They often provide opportunities for the faithful to experience a more intense communion."[38]
This "more intense communion" can also lead us to desire a deeper
relationship with Christ, creating a wonderful circle of deepening
engagement in a lifetime of faith. Small community group participants find church becoming an essential part of their lives, rather
than something that remains on the fringes of life. Members attend

Sunday Eucharist more regularly, consider Church teaching when making moral decisions in higher percentages than Catholics who are not part of a small group, and grow confident in praying aloud and leading others in prayer.[39]

Given the pace and pressure of the lives of many people, many parishes have found seasonal groups to be more inviting, especially initially, than a group that is ongoing. In the words of a parishioner who spoke about this at a parish meeting, "Many of the things I see in the bulletin sound like, 'Come, join our small group. We plan to meet every other week for the rest of your life.' I am not even sure what next week is going to be like, let alone 'the rest of my life'!" Still, finding ways to draw people in to small groups at least occasionally is an important element of engaging parish life. We will build on the idea of inviting people to intentionally connect with others in brief seasons in Section Two.

Of course, we know what happened at the end of the story of Jesus and the disciples on the beach. This small group of disciples who knew each other so well, and who supported one another amid confusion, hurt, and fear, sat with Jesus for breakfast on the beach. Jesus asked Peter "Do you love me?" and the one whom Jesus chose as the rock upon which our Church is built answered, "Yes, Lord, you know that I love you." Within this small group, the disciples experienced Jesus' love, mercy, and forgiveness. Like the disciples on the beach with our Lord, we who are disciples today need one another. We need to touch and hear and see the love of others in the name of Christ, and we need to be the same for someone else. There is nothing like a small group to make this possible, which leads us to our sixth Principle for Parish Life:

Principle Six: Become a community that **invites, encourages, and supports belonging to a small group**, fostering a living relationship with Christ through relationships with others.

Discovering and Dreaming: Your Parish's Life

DISCOVER *What opportunities exist in your parish for people to be part of a small group?*

What do you want to study further, reflect upon, or remember from this section?

DREAM *How might your parish encourage greater participation in small groups in the coming year?*

Key Themes for Pastoral Practice and Planning

Small Is Big

Build in Flexibility

(These themes are represented in the strategies found in Sections Two and Three)

CHAPTER SEVEN

Putting It Together

turning hearts to Christ

They devoted themselves to the apostles' teaching and fellowship, to the breaking of bread and the prayers. Awe came upon everyone, because many wonders and signs were being done by the apostles. All who believed were together and had all things in common; they would sell their possessions and goods and distribute the proceeds to all, as any had need. Day by day, as they spent much time together in the temple, they broke bread at home and ate their food with glad and generous hearts, praising God and having the goodwill of all the people. And day by day the Lord added to their number those who were being saved.

■ Acts 2:42–47

We break our pattern here of story, theological and research exploration, and considerations for pastoral practice because now it is time for you to begin to put this together in your own mind and heart, within your discussion groups, and work toward the beginnings of a plan. Here, the story, reflection, and practice are yours! This is a perfect moment to gather your discoveries and dreams from chapters one through six, to voice your questions, determine additional areas for study, and offer ideas for future consideration. We will use all that you bring to this moment in the process that is outlined in Section Three, but this is a good time in which to pause and take stock. As you do so, perhaps you might together state your own community's Principles for Parish Life. We will add one final, cumulative principle here, from which you might adapt, develop, or build upon:

Principle Seven: Become a community that **turns people's hearts to Christ, engaging them in a lifetime of faith.**

DISCOVER *What is already engaging people in a lifetime of faith within your parish?*

What is contributing to a deep sense of belonging among parishioners?

How does your parish meet people as they are, inviting them to real faith within your community?

In what ways do you already experience the outcomes of inviting, thanking, serving, and giving within your parish? What helps people to feel equipped to act on their engagement in these ways?

Through what intentional ways are people formed as disciples who express their relationship with Christ through stewardship and as evangelizing people?

What small group opportunities already exist within your parish?

> **DREAM** *together about a vision for the future of your parish that builds on all you have discovered thus far.*

We will return to your discovery and dreaming in Section Three. For now, perhaps a bit of synthesis with a few additional key points would be of benefit. As we take the research and our learning about belonging and combine it with our theological reflection, existing parish practice, and the experience of Catholic parishes that are already building engagement, there are a few essential thoughts to take with us into Section Two:

- **Belonging makes a difference!** The primary resource for the study of engagement is *Growing an Engaged Church* (see the bibliography for additional information). Within it, you will discover the steps that lead to engagement among parishioners. For the sake of this treatment we have focused on a greater awareness of the importance and impact of engaging parishioners, and we will next explore a strategy to build engagement through adult faith formation;

- **Put first things first!** Make the Eucharist central in the life of the parish, and people's lives at home will more easily fall into place;

- In order to enhance and increase the **centrality of the Eucharist** in people's hearts, lives, and actions, our **faith formation and parish life should flow from the Eucharist** rather than seeming to be extraneous to it;

- One of the key insights from the engagement studies is this: **Build on what is already working.** Do not focus on the absence of those who are rarely with us, or on the complaints of those who are always negative.[40] Instead, focus on what is already contributing to engaging pastoral practice in your parish, and build more effective, evangelizing life as a result. That is the reason for the adapted Appreciative Inquiry (AI) process. The work of those who have developed AI points to the same fundamental benefit of building on what is already working, especially by providing people an opportunity to tell their stories, hear the experience of others, and by doing so, to begin to see and to develop strategies for the future;

- The ways in which we relate with one another and with those who come to be among us must **be realistic and pastoral.** We want to reverence and value them as children of God. **At the same time we must encourage, expect, and challenge each member to grow in their commitment to Christ and the community of Christ, the Church;**

- Our **faith formation,** especially for youth and adults, can help to build engagement while **encouraging people to live as disciples** who are good **stewards** and who naturally **evangelize.** Experience shows that these same adults, as they become more engaged, will desire and willingly participate in faith formation that will lead them to greater knowledge of the faith, equipping them to live authentically as Catholic Christians in today's world;

- If we are to become a community in which people's hearts are turned to Christ for a lifetime, we must **intentionally help them to embrace ongoing conversion.**

Section Two

Seasonal Renewal for a Lifetime of Faith

We have thought about much in the previous section! Now it is time to draw together all we have learned and discussed to build a community that turns people's hearts to Christ. In conversation with pastoral leaders and parishioners, people often say, "Please, don't add one more thing! Our lives are more full now than we can handle." So, whatever we plan must be realistic for both leaders and the parishioners we serve. At the end of the last section, you began a positive process for evaluating what is already part of the life of your parish. You may have discovered a few practices, groups, processes, or programs that are no longer meeting the needs of parishioners. Needs do change, as do our people, and as do the circumstances of our life within our parishes. You may have also dreamt of new possibilities that would help to engage people more effectively. You will consider those again in the next section. For now, let us remember that whatever we do, we cannot simply tell ourselves or others that we are going to add a program or two to the already full life within our parishes and within the lives of our parishioners. That just will not work!

✍ Reinforce the Centrality of the Eucharist ✍

What can work, however, based on the experience of parishes of a variety of sizes and compositions, is to build relationships among parishioners, and orient your parish's entire life on the liturgical year, making the Eucharist central to our lives as individuals and within the community. Doing this immediately focuses our attention where it should be, just as we hope our people will do in their lives at home. With the feasts and seasons of our liturgical calendar in our mind's eye, we can easily identify particular moments in which we can focus people's attention toward and from the Eucharist and sacramental life of the Church by intentionally inviting people into opportunities for spiritual renewal and growth. Using the liturgical seasons as the foundation for spiritual formation for youth and adults provides a rhythm and pace to life that is the Church's very own. We reinforce the most important aspects of our Catholic life together, and we help people to take this to their homes, their workplaces, neighborhoods, city or town, and world.

Renew Hearts and Minds

Next, people in today's culture are often over-stimulated, torn among competing priorities, and aching for something that will bring them focus, peace, and purpose. Whatever we do, then, must take this real and pressing need into account. In his letter to the Romans, St. Paul offers guidance that rings true today: "I appeal to you, therefore, brothers and sisters, by the mercies of God, to present your bodies as a living sacrifice, holy and acceptable to God, which is your spiritual worship. Do not be conformed to this world, but be transformed by the renewing of your minds, so that you may discern what is the will of God—what is good and acceptable and perfect" (Romans 12:1–2). St. Paul is right: We need to be transformed by being renewed. If there is anything today's Catholic youth and adults need, it is renewal! When we allow God to re-create us, we are transformed; we are more able to put the competing pressures and influences of our lives in perspective and discern God's will for our lives. Our true spiritual needs will be met, and our lives will come into clearer focus, with greater meaning for our future.

Engage People in Living Discipleship

Third, we have already established that the strategies we will consider here will have as a foundation the desire to engage people in living discipleship, leading them to live as stewards, and encouraging them to be evangelized and evangelizing. Again, the experience of pastoral leaders and parishioners tells us that youth and adults will respond to meaningful occasions of renewal and formation to encounter and be encountered by Christ through timely, realistic, and pastoral catechesis. Even more, once people experience faith formation that truly fits their lives, they will ask for more, they will desire deeper spiritual formation, they will want to know more of what we believe and why, and they will offer their help in bringing to reality the kind of formation they truly want and need. All we have to do is "prime the pump" by providing the foundation of seasonal moments of renewal, and the rest will begin to fall into place.

✑ Seasonal Renewal ✑

With these things in mind, consider how wonderful it could be to engage people for a lifetime of faith by inviting them to participate in Seasonal Renewal each year. Each season is connected to the liturgical life of the Church, is realistic and pastoral, and can meet the needs of members who are already engaged, not engaged, or who have fallen into active disengagement. Your seasonal contact with parishioners can be varied in style and structure, and people can embrace the seasonal focus points in all of the facets of their lives and in ways that meet their needs. None is too long, and each leads individuals, families, and the community to embrace lifelong conversion in Christ. For those who are already deeply engaged, the liturgical seasons are so much a part of our lives that the processes suggested here will feel familiar. Yet, each carries with it the potential to be transformative, not just once, but over and over again, as we fall more deeply in love with Christ each season, within our parishes, and within our very lives.

Each seasonal renewal period builds on the Sunday Eucharist, celebrated with care, and intentionally coordinated to draw people's prayerful attention to the richness of the season. The renewal may include any or all of the following elements of spiritual formation; each season will employ a slightly different combination of elements to more fully reflect the season's focus:

1. A Pre-Season meeting in which people are introduced to, reminded of, or become more fully immersed in the season's themes and through which they become more deeply connected to each other;

2. A brief statement or question for reflection, tied to the Sunday readings;

3. Opportunities for people to serve and reach out to others, through coordinated projects or by making local needs known to parishioners;

4. Encouragement to prayerfully read sacred Scripture and to keep a prayer and Scripture journal;

5. Invitation or greeting cards for parishioners to share with their family and friends;

6. Weekly articles or prayers in the parish bulletin or website;

7. Opportunities for people to share their faith with others in small groups, dyads, and at home.

None of these elements seems like much by itself, but together, they form the basis for a season of enhanced spirituality, increased connection with the faith community, and the likelihood of growth in spiritual commitment and the outcomes of inviting, thanking, serving, and giving. By establishing many points of contact with parishioners throughout the season, you will increase your parish's ability to reach out to people in meaningful ways, building a lasting sense of belonging that will lead them to turn their hearts to Christ.

Here is a chart that provides an overview of the seasons, with their key theological themes and practical focus points. In what follows we will delve more deeply into each season, explore the theological underpinnings, focuses for renewal, and discipleship-action/outcome connections.

ADVENT / CHRISTMAS		
Theological Focus	**Renewal Focus**	**Key Theme**
Incarnation	Reverence people, family, community ***Personal or family renewal*** Connect faith to life and people to the parish	"God is with us"
This season leads to:	Inviting	"Here, we belong and we invite you to belong"
LENT / EASTER		
Theological Focus	**Renewal Focus**	**Key Theme**
Passion, death, resurrection	Metanoia, prayer, fasting, works of charity / almsgiving ***Spiritual renewal*** Turn hearts to Christ again or for the first time	"Christ calls, Christ loves"
This season leads to:	Thanking	"Here, together our hearts are turned to Christ"

ORDINARY TIME		
Theological Focus	**Renewal Focus**	**Key Theme**
Discipleship, living relationship	Following Christ for a lifetime of faith **Discipleship or stewardship renewal** Caring and sharing in the footsteps of Jesus	"We respond, we call, we serve"
This season leads to:	Serving and giving	"Here, we have found meaning; come stand with us on holy ground"

As you can see from the table above, by focusing our attention on the rhythm of the liturgical year, we can easily draw people into a lifetime of faith through seasonal renewal. We can focus on the theological themes of the seasons and invite people to embrace the discipleship actions that naturally follow as a result. What is more, if we orient and focus the rest of our parish's life in relationship to the liturgy, our lives will feel more congruent and less distracted. The elements of life within our parish will take on deeper meaning, we will be more likely to engage people in lasting and meaningful ways, and we will be more able to turn people's hearts to Christ as a result.

"God Is With Us"

"Joseph, son of David, do not be afraid to take Mary as your wife, for the child conceived in her is from the Holy Spirit. She will bear a son, and you are to name him Jesus, for he will save his people from their sins." All this took place to fulfill what had been spoken by the Lord through the prophet: "Look, the virgin shall conceive and bear a son and they shall name him Emmanuel, which means, 'God is with us.'" When Joseph awoke from sleep, he did as the angel of the Lord commanded him; he took her as his wife, but had no marital relations with her until she had borne a son, and he named him Jesus. ■ Matthew 1:20b–25

☙ Theological Focus ❧

Oh, to be surrounded by people like Joseph! Joseph, who faced a moral dilemma with faith, who listened to the voice of the Lord, who acted on his relationship with God in trust, and whose witness and action inspire us even today. The seasons of Advent and Christmas are filled with so many wonderful images and stories of faith: Isaiah, John, Mary, and Joseph among them. Becoming spiritually and prayerfully immersed in Advent and Christmas helps us to understand in a deep way that "God is with us." Our lives take on greater meaning when we think about what this means for our relationship with Christ and our daily interactions with others. What does it mean for us that God so desires to be with us that God came to be one with us in Christ? How do our lives make the wonder and awe of the incarnation more clearly visible to others?

Yet we know that for most of our parishioners, Advent has become something that is only marked on Sunday at Mass, or perhaps through an Advent wreath at home that rarely gets lit. The weeks leading up to Christmas have become the "Christmas season" in the lives and minds of most of our people, and the days following Christmas are, well, back to the "ordinary." Our lives at home are out of sync with our liturgical life, and yet it is the liturgy with the rhythm of feasts and seasons that is to shape the rhythm of our daily lives. The seasons that immerse us more deeply into Christ's Paschal Mystery have developed over the centuries for just these very reasons. The Church in her wisdom knows that we need preparation in order to encounter the deep mystery of Christ's incarnational love. Not only that, the beginning of the season of Advent asks us to take stock of our lives, to think about where we stand in relationship to the hopes and expectations God has for us, and to anticipate a time in which we will meet God face to face. These are not things to be taken lightly or to miss in the busy pace of shopping, planning for family visits, and the requisite Christmas pageant or concert!

Practical Considerations

Yet, most parishes that attempt anything beyond an occasional, brief gathering during Advent meet with sparse participation at best. Our parishioners will say very clearly: "What I really don't need is something else to do this month," and in some sense, they're probably right. What they do need, what we all need, are ways to reflect on the richness of all that Advent and Christmas spread before us, within the context of our real lives, with all their busy pace, demands, and responsibilities, and the anticipation that is part of the season.

Renewing People and Families

Rather than taking either the stance of "don't give people what they don't want" and therefore providing nothing more than Mass during Advent and Christmas, or the stance of "why can't people see that they need more than what they're willing to do?" perhaps we can instead find ways to offer one another the possibility of real personal or family renewal. What if the parish became the community that expresses reverence for each member by helping them to reflect, pray, and live the incarnational love of God for each of us? Invite parishioners to participate in a pre-Advent meeting in late Autumn, leading up to the season of Advent. Then, ask each person to make a commitment to open their minds and hearts to be renewed during Advent and Christmas, and promise them that this renewal is more qualitative than quantitative. Assure them that your greatest hope is that their lives will be filled with a new awareness of and appreciation for the gift of Christ in this season of gift giving. This is a gift that will never need to be returned, and one that can be opened again and again!

✑ Connecting Faith with Real Life... ◈

Inviting parishioners to participate in seasonal renewal during Advent and Christmas—renewal that draws from the Sunday Eucharist and is connected to their life at home—will provide the deeper immersion people need in a format and structure that they will appreciate. Furthermore, offering people something that truly reverences them and helps them to recognize the sacredness within all that is part of their lives (including the messiness, turmoil, mixed feelings about family gatherings, and all that other stressful stuff that many experience—more during this season than at any other time of the year) will help people to establish a rhythm of life that has as its foundation an abiding relationship with Christ.

✑ ...and Life to the Parish ◈

What is more, many families have special traditions that they bring with them from their culture of origin. Acknowledging, reverencing, and connecting these to the community will help people feel a new sense of belonging within the parish family. Traditions such as St. Nicholas' feast, the feast of Our Lady of Guadalupe, Las Posadas, the blessing of the crèche, special food, and carols all carry with them elements of the story of God's love for us, brought to fullness in Christ, and lived on in the Body of Christ, the Church.

Connecting our traditions of the season at home with their greater meaning through the parish is sure to bring people to a heightened appreciation for both.

ᔟ This Season Will Lead to... ᔦ

Inviting: "Here, we belong, and we invite you to belong."

When our parishes become places in which we truly feel we are reverenced and where we belong, we naturally want to bring others to the community. During Advent, many families plan their Christmas celebrations. Personal and family spiritual renewal in this season can lead people to invite their family members and friends with them to Christmas Mass, to winter or spring events at the parish, or simply into conversation about the most important things in their lives: their relationship with God and how they are (or are not) growing in that relationship at this time. By inviting people to participate in a season of personal and family renewal, we can lead people to say to those they love, "Here, we belong and we invite you to belong with us."

ᔟ What This Season of Renewal Looks Like ᔦ

The Advent/Christmas Renewal may include:

Personal or Family Reflection: Provide a pre-season reflection at the parish in the late autumn, helping parishioners to become immersed in Advent and Christmas at home. Then, throughout the seasons of Advent and Christmas as we are being dismissed from Sunday Mass, invite people to pay particular attention to the flyer or column in the bulletin in the coming week. (You might even eliminate all other announcements for the season, except perhaps those important Mass time announcements as we approach Christmas!) Offer a look at the seasonal themes in relationship to our lives at home, work, and in our community. Remember that these need to be particularly focused on bringing the themes of the season to life in brief, realistic, and relational ways. Focus the development of the reflections in the parish bulletin or website on those who come to Mass but are not already connected. Those who are engaged will use them, of course, and they will also share them with those in their circles who have little place for faith in their lives. Use a tone in your written and spoken communication that is more like talking with family or good friends than talking to strangers.

Prayer: Many parishes take time in Advent for the celebration of the sacrament of reconciliation. If this is part of your parish's sacramental life, enhance it by inviting parishioners to prepare through an examination of their lives that is reflective of the season. Spend time at Mass, just after Mass, or in the Sunday bulletin in the weeks prior to your reconciliation celebration to help parishioners to prepare their minds and hearts.

Connect Cultural Traditions: Invite people to share their traditional customs, food, songs, and stories with the community. If your parish is blessed with many ethnic groups, invite each group to organize a simple gathering for the rest of the community; or invite all of the members to bring something to share to a community pot-luck (some might bring food, others a song, others the table or room decorations). Provide parishioners with a calendar that weaves in all of the special feasts that have been embraced by various cultural groups within the seasons of Advent and Christmas, and feature them in the parish newsletter with stories from parish families that illustrate the deeper meaning of the season. Or, invite people to share their customs and traditions in brief gatherings following Sunday Mass.

Give Parishioners Invitation Cards they can share with their family and friends, listing the times and other appropriate details for the Christmas liturgies. Plan, too, to warmly welcome visitors, and have some simple gift or gathering designed just for them for the weeks following Christmas. Perhaps a prayer card with the parish's name, address, and contact information, can be shared with everyone who comes. Or, offer a gathering for people who have been away from the practice of our faith for a time. This is a simple way of equipping the engaged to invite others to turn their hearts to Christ.

"Christ Calls, Christ Loves"

They urged him, "Stay with us, for it is nearly eve-
ning and the day is almost over." So he went in to
stay with them. And it happened that, while he
was with them at table, he took bread, said the
blessing, broke it, and gave it to them. With that
their eyes were opened and they recognized him,
but he vanished from their sight. Then they said to
each other, "Were not our hearts burning within
us while he spoke to us on the way and opened the
Scriptures to us?" ■ Luke 24:29–32

✓ Theological Focus ✓

This beloved passage from the Gospel of Luke gives us in encapsulated form all the hopes that we expressed at the beginning of this book. Jesus so loved the disciples with whom he journeyed, that, while amazed at their doubts and confusion, he unfolded for them the fullness of who he is, culminating in their gathering at table where "he was made known to them in the breaking of bread" (Luke 24:35). In this encounter, our Lord met the disciples as they are, and Christ meets us where we are, "across time and space to each human being, each mind, each heart." Through this passage, we are asked "what we think about our lives, how we hope, whom we love and what we live for."[41] Real lives, real people, real faith, real presence! As pastoral leaders who want to engage people in a lifetime of faith, we yearn for all people to have burning hearts, filled with the love of Christ, for Christ, and for the world. The seasons of Lent and Easter help us to reflect on all that being baptized into Christ's death and resurrection means for us, and this mystery, this paschal mystery, is one that truly takes a lifetime to live!

Still, many, perhaps most, of our parishioners barely skim the surface of the great saving love of Christ that we encounter in Lent and Easter. For many, Lent begins and ends on Ash Wednesday, or is fulfilled by "giving up" some non-essential food or activity, giving at least the impression of observation of the season. If Easter is celebrated, it is as likely to include bunnies and fashion as any real exploration of faith in Christ and our Christian life. Again, our lives at home are markedly out of sync with our liturgical life, and, again, the liturgy holds that which is to shape and mold, nourish and strengthen, challenge and console our life in faith. Lent calls us to metanoia, to turn our hearts to Christ again or for the first time; the traditional practices of prayer, fasting, and works of charity or almsgiving help us to focus our lives so that we more genuinely mirror the love of Christ. By challenging ourselves and one another to connect our daily dyings and risings with that of Christ, we find hope, peace, and the reason to live more fully as Christ's own.

✍ Practical Considerations ✎

The good news in the season of Lent and Easter is that most Catholics are attuned to Lent in ways they are not to other liturgical seasons. Most adults have in their memory special lenten practices at home; they have participated in lenten missions or retreat days; they know that violet is the color of the season, and many have traditions of weaving palm, eating fish, and praying the Way of the Cross. We can build on this heritage of lenten practice to invite people to a seasonal renewal during Lent and Easter that is sure to reap a rich harvest in their lives and the life of the community.

✍ Spiritual Renewal ✎

A growing number of adults in our era live by the premise that "I am spiritual, but not religious." In other words, "I have a spiritual life that does not require institutional religion." The younger the adult, the more likely this notion will be a guiding principle. Bookstores are filled with titles that treat "spirituality," and yet, we know that many of these treatments are lacking in substance. Still, knowing that many of our parishioners are just shy of "spiritual but not religious" (they do attend church, but that is the extent of the connection for them between a relationship with God and participation as a member of Christ's Body) provides an opportunity to invite people to be renewed in spirit during Lent and Easter. This season of spiritual renewal will invite people to peer deeply into their own lives in relationship with Christ, the Church, to name their spiritual needs in their own minds and hearts, and to embrace living discipleship that bears the fruit of service, solidarity with the poor, advocating for justice, longing for peace, and bringing others to Christ.

Connecting Faith with Real Life...

Knowing that many among us feel a need for a deeper spiritual life, and recognizing that for many of us the pace of life seems to become continually faster,[42] a season of spiritual renewal during Lent and Easter is a means for meeting people as they are, quenching an unnamed and often un- or under-recognized thirst. This spiritual renewal will bring those previously not engaged in a growing life of discipleship to a new willingness to respond to Christ's call and Christ's love.

...and Life to the Parish

While the suggestion during the Advent/Christmas season of renewal was to connect people's lives to the parish by reverencing what they experience at home and to connect it to the greater story of faith through the parish, this season will be different. The suggestion for Lent/Easter is to invite people to begin with a pre-season meeting that will encourage their participation in the traditional lenten spiritual practices of prayer, fasting, and almsgiving or works of charity, helping them to name and to find in Christ the fulfillment of every spiritual need they perceive in their heart, now and into eternity. People can be encouraged to prayerfully read sacred Scripture through a practice such as lectio divina; they can be given a simple journal or questions for deeper spiritual reflection; and they can be invited into an intentional partnership with another, joining companions on the spiritual journey who will encourage one another's steadfastness and challenge each other to continued growth.

✎ This Season Will Lead to... ✎

Thanking: "Here, together our hearts are turned to Christ."

When our community draws us to turn our hearts to Christ again or for the first time, we are filled with gratitude for the saving, forgiving, merciful, and compelling love of our God for us, and our lives are transformed. This is not surface change, like "giving up" candy for Lent! This is metanoia, the turning of our lives toward Christ in a way that is substantial and lasting. Change such as this causes us to mirror Christ's love to others, so that they experience forgiveness, mercy, and the compelling love of God through us. By inviting people to participate in a season of spiritual renewal, they will find themselves saying to others, in their words or their actions, "Here, together our hearts are turned to Christ. Come and see what a difference this can make."

✎ What This Season of Renewal Looks Like ✎

The Lent/Easter Season of Renewal may include

A Pre-Season Small Group Mini-Retreat: At the parish or in people's homes, invite parishioners to explore the riches of God's love for us in Christ through the Spirit. The mini-retreat, or a day-long retreat at the parish, offers parishioners an occasion of prayer and reflection that brings the season to life by making lasting connections between Christ's Paschal Mystery and the daily moments of our own lives. These experiences will be connected to the Sunday celebration of the Eucharist, infusing their lives with the spiritual renewal that Lent and Easter help us to experience. Consider sending parishioners an email or postal mailing just prior to Lent inviting them to participate and asking them to invite a friend or family member to come as well.

Fasting and Almsgiving or Works of Mercy: Invite parishioners to make the traditional lenten practices their own by writing down and/ or sharing their commitments with another. Ritualize this commitment-making within the Ash Wednesday liturgy or during the Pre-Season gathering.

Prayer: Most parishes include the sacrament of reconciliation during Lent, and some also have a pattern of weekly Evening or Morning Prayer. The mini-retreat can lead people to participate in reconciliation, or other occasions of prayer, so be prepared for more participants than might be typical, welcome them warmly, and encourage their return.

"We Respond, We Call, We Serve"

*Brothers and sisters: No one can say, "Jesus is Lord,"
except by the Holy Spirit. There are different kinds
of spiritual gifts but the same Spirit; there are different forms of service but the same Lord; there
are different workings but the same God who pro-
duces all of them in everyone. To each individual
the manifestation of the Spirit is given for some
benefit. As a body is one though it has many parts,
and all the parts of the body, though many, are
one body, so also Christ. For in one Spirit we were
all baptized into one body, whether Jew or Greeks,
slaves or free persons, and we were all given to
drink of one Spirit.* ▪ 1 Corinthians 12:3b–7, 12–13

❧ Theological Focus ❧

At baptism we were immersed into Christ's death and life and anointed with the Holy Spirit. In confirmation we were sealed with the fullness of that same Spirit, sent to live as God's very own in the world. Ordinary time, that counted time that comprises much of each year, invites us to respond to Christ's call, in turn to bear Christ's invitation to others, and to serve in love as a witness to Christ's love for all. This call to and for Christ is the call of our lives, the call that gives all other calls (to relationship, to work, to a particular type of service or ministry) meaning. The dynamic rhythm of the liturgical seasons and feasts sends us from Advent and Christmas to Ordinary Time and from Ordinary Time to Lent and Easter and back to Ordinary Time again each year. The cycles of readings, liturgical colors, theological and pastoral focus points of each season, all of this is intended to bring us ever more deeply to the heart of Christ and out to the world in Christ's name, for God's greater glory. We leave Easter, for instance, with the feast of Pentecost, and we are reminded that the Spirit of God was not given to the early believers in a one-time-only offer, but rather that the Holy Spirit was poured out on the early believers, the Church, once and for all ages, and upon each of us for our lifetime into eternity. There is nothing "ordinary" about that!

Yet most of the people in our parishes, if they even know the phrase "Ordinary Time," do consider it to be "ordinary." People look at the repetitious nature of the ritual elements of the liturgy and they see "ordinary"; they hear announcements at Mass inviting them to participate in some event, organization, or process, and they hear "ordinary." They remain numb to the grace of each celebration and each moment because they fail to recognize Christ's call to them as a beloved child of God. They cannot see themselves as possessing any real gifts that might be of benefit to others. And they do not believe anyone would miss them if they stopped coming, or care if they continue as they are, by coming to Mass but not connecting with us in any meaningful way. And they are right. The not-engaged among us are not negative; they are simply waiting to be drawn more deeply to Christ through the community. They are also more likely to slip away, into the flow of people who just disappear. And the majority of the people in our parishes are not engaged. The overwhelming majority are not engaged or actively disengaged.

Ordinary time is our great opportunity to bring people to a living relationship with Christ that lasts for a lifetime. It is the time in which we hear reading after reading, Sunday after Sunday, describe for us who disciples are and what disciples do. We do not need to hammer people over the head with it, instilling what is colloquially known as "Catholic guilt." Rather, like Christ, who said to the first disciples, "Come and see," we can invite parishioners and those whom they bring into a living relationship that has room to grow, to deepen, and to flourish. As an older and experienced monsignor once told a younger pastor, "Keep doing what you are doing; preach the whole gospel."

✑ Practical Considerations ✎

While many parishes do adjust their daily and weekly rhythm during Advent, Christmas, Lent, and Easter, it is during Ordinary Time that parishes often either become hyper-active, seemingly unfocused and not connected to the liturgy, or hypo-active, falling into a quiet and contented lull. Neither seems totally appropriate if we want our parishes to be places in which we engage people for a lifetime of faith. The lifetime not only includes those "special" seasons and "high holy days," but rather the accumulation of all of the days, weeks, months, and years of our lives. Perhaps it is time to evaluate all of the activity that takes place at your parish to consider the benefits and blessings provided as a result. It might be that a little focus is all that is needed, or everything may be just as it should be; every parish has a different combination of factors and needs to be taken into account. As you begin to map out the year, let us consider one additional season of renewal.

✒ Discipleship or Stewardship Renewal ✑

Parishes that are already fostering a spirituality of stewardship often have some particular moment, usually during Ordinary Time, in which people are invited to commit themselves as disciples and stewards. There is much benefit to such a practice, even more when we take into consideration all that we have learned about engagement and the discipleship-actions or outcomes of engagement. Inviting people into a Season of Discipleship or Stewardship Renewal will help them focus on what it means to belong to Christ and on their call to follow Jesus "no matter the cost to themselves." As a season of renewal, this is more than words on paper. This is a season in which people are asked to allow Christ to challenge them, as Jesus challenged those he encountered in the gospels. We each need to take time every year to think about how we respond to Christ's call to follow him as a disciple, as one who is learning the Master's Way. What gifts have we been given as a child who is uniquely and wonderfully created in God's image? In what ways do we feel called to develop those gifts and give them back with increase? Without the annual season of renewal, it is easy to slip into the delusion that we are doing what we could or should. With an annual Season of Discipleship or Stewardship Renewal, we commit or recommit ourselves in a real way to the life that Jesus calls us to live. We are called to care and to share as one who walks in the footsteps of Jesus.

✍ Connecting Faith with Real Life... ✎

Asking parishioners to participate in a Season of Discipleship or Stewardship Renewal is all about connecting faith with real life. It is a time for each person to look at the connection between his or her relationship with Christ and to think about what that relationship calls him or her to be or to do. In many ways this Season of Discipleship or Stewardship Renewal is about that phrase we have considered previously from the bishops' letter on evangelization: the season will ask each of us: "How does the Gospel speak to your mind and your heart? What do you think about your life? For what do you hope? Whom do you love? What do you live for? If your faith is not transforming your heart and life, it is dead!"

✍ ...and Life to the Parish ✎

And it is in the parish that faith is nurtured and that faith grows. Parishes that engage members in a real and living relationship with Jesus Christ—lived out in discipleship that is expressed in stewardship and in natural evangelization—are parishes that fulfill Christ's call to live as people of mission. Such communities truly turn people's hearts to Christ by engaging them in a lifetime of faith.

✍ This Season will Lead to... ✎

Serving and Giving: "Here, we have found meaning; come stand with us on holy ground."

When people truly understand themselves as disciples, their lives take on much greater meaning than they imagined possible. They see themselves as being given particular gifts that are needed in our world. They recognize that without their love and service, something will be missing. They also come to understand, as Sam did in our earlier story, that they have a need to give, and they respond out of love for God and others. They come to see the parish as a place in which each person is a valued member, and they naturally desire that their disconnected, not engaged, or actively disengaged family and friends discover what is giving their lives such great meaning. They serve and give willingly "without counting the cost to themselves," and they say to others, through their lives and witness, their attitudes and actions: "Here we have found meaning, come stand with us on holy ground."

✍ What This Season of Renewal Looks Like ✎

The Ordinary Time Season of Renewal may include:

Discipleship Renewal, Two by Two: Discipleship is not something that is undertaken alone, a "me and Jesus thing." Rather it is something that is experienced and that grows within relationships with other Christians. Jesus sent disciples out in pairs, and we can nurture and help our parishioners to live as disciples by encouraging them to participate in a season of renewal with another. Start by inviting people to participate in a special Season of Renewal in which they will come closer to our Lord and to others. Gather people together for a "Two by Two" meet and greet. Encourage people to pair up with someone they do not already know. This will help them to become more closely tied to the community. Or, invite couples to pair with a couple they do not yet know, strengthening both the family and the community. Start the process with a service day (already organized and promoted in advance), or give participants a list of local service opportunities, within the parish and in the local community. Provide pairs with conversation prompts, and suggest that they serve together at least once in a six-week period, and that they commit to meeting together once each week for that same six weeks. Pairs may elect to stay together, meeting once a month after Sunday Mass or at a different time once they have become acquainted, or they may join a different pair for the next Two by Two Discipleship Renewal.

Stewardship Renewal: If your parish already has a period set aside each year for stewardship renewal, take that time to also help people to reflect on how belonging leads them to invite, to thank, to serve, and to give. For a sample of such stewardship reflection, see the Samples page at www.thegenerousheart.com. If your parish does not already have such a time, this may be a point of development for the future. Stewardship renewal seasons often include a parish report of financial and ministerial giving for the previous year, a ministry or service fair, lay witnesses, culminating in a reflection on our lives as disciples and stewards with a written commitment. The Two by Two Discipleship Renewal could be part of your annual stewardship renewal effort.

Service Days: Many parishes organize service Saturdays in which people gather, pray, participate in a common service project (or multiple projects if enough people commit to participate), return for reflection on the experience, participate in the anticipatory Mass on Saturday evening, and enjoy a simple supper together. This is a great way to invite those who are not deeply connected to take an initial leap of faith and to put their faith into action.

Section Three

An Appreciative Process for Development and Planning

Y ou have already begun to gather your discoveries and dreams, recording them in Sections One and Two and discussing them with your group. Now it is time to prayerfully consider all you have read, studied, discussed, and thought about individually and within your group(s), pulling together the strands of conversation toward a plan for the future. This planning stage is absolutely crucial to what we have considered previously. To quote a fitting maxim, "If we fail to plan, we plan to fail." We may not fail in the sense that we will continue to celebrate the sacraments and interact with each other in our parish, but it is true that if we do not intentionally develop a plan for what we have considered previously, it is doubtful that our reading and discussion will lead to any real, transformative change.

✎ A Step-by-Step Path for Planning ✍

Your planning will be most effective by following these steps:

1. Collect your **Discoveries** and **Dreams** from your learning, thought, and discussions during Sections One and Two;

2. **Discern** next steps that will lead you to fulfill your dreams together;

3. **Design an Initial Plan** that will guide the development of a longer-term plan following additional input gathering and time to implement some concrete strategies such as the Seasonal Renewal;

4. **Determine** when to gather qualitative and quantitative input from parishioners (more on this below);

5. **Design** a longer-term plan to guide your parish's life for the future.

The planning process that follows is an adaptation of Appreciative Inquiry (see bibliography for additional information). This process will help you to name what is already contributing positively to your parish's life, and to build on that toward engaging people in a lifetime of faith. This process can be used in any situation that necessitates decision making, and is particularly fitting for our work with engagement, since it helps us to build on what is already working in our parishes.

Use the Appreciative Process now, to develop an Initial Plan for your parish, taking into account your thoughts, discussions, and study based on *Turning Hearts to Christ*. In your plan, identify areas in which input from parishioners will be of great benefit, for instance, to gain parishioners' insights, questions, and desires for your liturgical celebrations or to hear people's hopes for catechesis for them and their children or grandchildren. There are two types of input that can be acquired, both with the potential to help you create an engaging parish for a lifetime of faith together.

◦ Qualitative and Quantitative Input ◦

Depending on your parish's previous experience with evaluation and planning, its current circumstances, and your commitment to engage people in a lifetime of faith, inviting parishioners to offer their input in some intentional and strategic way can greatly enhance the possibility that your parish will grow in the ways we have discussed.

The ME25: Quantitative Input through a Parish-Wide Engagement Survey: Parishes throughout the United States and Canada are experiencing substantial renewal by measuring engagement through a survey developed by the Gallup Organization called the "ME25." The ME25, which stands for "Member Engagement, 25 questions" is a brief survey that all adult parishioners complete. Based in the extensive research conducted by Gallup on parishioner engagement, the survey and summary report gives parish leaders an in-depth understanding of the ways in which parishioners do or do not sense that they belong. With this understanding, they are able to adjust parish practices, develop an annual engagement plan, and manage the aspects of parish life to contribute to an increase in engagement over time. The Appendix includes contact information to acquire details on the ME25, its potential benefits for your parish, and the time and financial commitment involved.

The Two by Two Project: Qualitative Input through Active Listening: By actively listening to parishioners' experiences and building parish life that will meet their needs, you will be assured that the practices you develop or those you retain will most effectively engage people now and into the future. Parishes that have reached out to parishioners to actively listen to them, using a method such as the "Two by Two Project" have seen a dramatic transformation in their parish's life and mission. Developed by Bill Huebsch, the Two by Two Project sends pastoral council or other listening leaders out into the community with the intention that people's hopes and needs will be heard. By actively listening in this way, not only are needs identified, but parishioners develop a sense that the parish truly is a caring community, one in which our "brothers and sisters in the faith so regard one another as those who are a part of me."

Gathering input insures that your parish's plan is not based solely on the perceptions of deeply involved leaders such as yourself. It is important that we hear and acknowledge the desires, hopes, dreams, and expectations of those who are not yet familiar to us. With all that we have considered in Sections One and Two, it seems appropriate to gather input in at least four essential elements:

Sunday Eucharist and Your Parish's Sacramental and Liturgical Life:
The fullness of our lives as Catholic Christians is expressed, deepened, and nourished in the celebration of the Eucharist and in our sacramental life. It is important that we take the time to prepare the liturgy with care, to insure that we are praying as the Church guides and directs, and also to ensure that the people who gather will most readily encounter, and be encountered by, our Lord through our liturgical prayer. Much of what we have learned and discussed in this book is aimed at helping people to be predisposed to the mysteries we celebrate when we gather for the liturgy. It is also crucial, however, to take stock of our liturgical life, to hear people's questions, reflections, and desires, and to understand as much as possible the ways in which the celebration of the Sunday Eucharist and sacraments helps to engage people in living faith. Actively listening to parishioners will provide the concrete input you need in order to know how people are being reached and touched through the liturgy.

Catechesis: We have focused much of our learning and discussion in this book on the ways our parish life helps to engage people in a lifetime of faith. Gathering input from a variety of parishioners, at various ages and stages of their lives and faith, will ensure that the strategies you develop will most effectively meet their needs and encourage their growth as disciples.

Stewardship: Inviting and expecting that people will express their relationship with Christ by giving of themselves and their resources helps people to more fully appreciate how their faith meets their real life. Hearing their struggles, facing with them their hesitations, and encouraging their commitment will best be accomplished through a process of active listening. This will help you to develop realistic and effective strategies to encourage further growth in the future.

Parish Life: There are so many ways in which our parish communities can help people to feel that they belong, leading them to be committed to our Lord and to others. Listening to their hopes and dreams, desires and concerns is a sure way to build engagement in lasting and powerful ways.

Information on resources to guide the Two by Two Project, with particular focuses on parish life, the liturgy, catechesis, and stewardship, is also included at the end of this section.

While the Two by Two Project primarily involves an investment in time and attention, the ME25 involves an investment in time and financial resources. The investments will bear great fruit, however, because this input-gathering will greatly enhance your parish's ability to engage people for the life of individuals and ultimately transform your community to turn people's hearts to Christ.

ᢟ Building Your Initial Plan ᢠ

Your discussion and development of an initial plan will require at least one meeting of as many of the leaders who have read and studied *Turning Hearts to Christ* as you are able to gather. You may decide to schedule two meetings for this, or you might gather the group together for the first meeting, appoint a sub-committee to discern appropriate next steps and to design a draft plan, and then call the whole group back together to finalize your initial plan.

It is time now to develop your Initial Plan.

An Appreciative Process for Planning and Development

Take a few moments to settle in silence and invite the Holy Spirit to be with you as you dream of an engaging future for your parish:

> *Holy Spirit, Fire of Love,*
> *Open our hearts and minds to your wisdom;*
> > *Come, Holy Spirit!*
> *Guide our community as we walk the ways of discipleship;*
> > *Come, Holy Spirit!*
> *Give us courage to serve boldly and with compassion;*
> > *Come, Holy Spirit!*
> *Strengthen our faith as we grow more deeply in relationship*
> *with Christ and one another;*
> > *Come, Holy Spirit!*
> *Enliven us in your presence, for you are God, with the Father*
> *and the Son, now and forever.*
> > *Come, Holy Spirit, come!*
> *Amen.*

Collect Your Discoveries and Dreams

In clusters of two or three, share the discoveries and dreams that you recorded in Section One, or things that came to mind as you read Section Two. Summarize these for the larger group; eliminate redundancies by creating statements that reflect the common focus of comments or observations.

Then, within your whole group, collect your discoveries and dreams together.

✒ Discern Your Future Direction ✒

Let your discoveries and dreams lead you to discern ways you may build on what is already working, developing a plan to fulfill your dreams. If there are too many dreams to be reasonable, take time to reach some consensus on the three or four dreams that are of the greatest potential and importance. Remember: consensus does not mean the majority rules, rather consensus leads us to consider what is of the greatest potential benefit for the community.

In this discernment, consider: What resources, experiences, and gifts do you have within your community that will contribute to the fulfillment of the dreams? In other words, how are the dreams attainable?

✒ Design a Plan ✒

Now, design a plan that will lead you to act on the strategies and steps you identified in your discernment. You may appoint a sub-committee to develop the plan for the group's later review and approval. The plan needs to be laid out in timeline form and it should list the people who will be responsible or who will coordinate the various aspects of the plan. This initial plan should include the steps you will take to acquire parishioner input directed toward specific elements of parish life in the future, and should make provision for the creation of a long-term plan after this input has been gathered.

DISCOVER: What is already engaging people in a lifetime of faith within your parish?

DREAM: What vision do you dream of together for the future of your parish?

DISCERN: How will you build on what is already working to move toward your dream? What resources, experiences, and gifts do you have within your community that will contribute to the fulfillment of your dreams?

DESIGN: Create a plan to make your dream a reality. Include a projected timeline, the point persons for each step, and any additional considerations to be taken into account.

Engaging People in the Liturgy

Does the way we celebrate the liturgy serve as a bridge between the immense love of God and the real lives of people?

Or do we, through our actions, words, or lack of them, heighten the perception of a wall between the liturgical action and the people who gather (and therefore a separation between the people and God, who will always love them)?

Do we help people to understand and to reflect upon our liturgical prayer so that their lives may be shaped by the mysteries we celebrate in the Eucharist and the sacraments?

In what ways do our pastoral and liturgical practices engage people in the liturgy and so engage them in Christ's life and love?

Throughout this book we have recognized the central role of the liturgy in the lives of individuals and in the life of the community. We have seen that people who are engaged are more likely to be thankful people whose very lives express the deep gratitude that is at the heart of what we celebrate in the Eucharist. We also know that the more engaged the community becomes, the more powerfully people will embrace Christ's call to believe and live the fullness of all that God intends in our world. The more deeply engaged people are within the community of faith, the more powerfully Christ's presence is known and perceived when the community gathers, since the people who gather know themselves as members of Christ's Body, the Church.

What we have not touched upon until now is the way in which our communal prayer can help to engage people more deeply in Christ's life and in the community of faith. This brief section will invite you to consider your parish's liturgical practices in light of all we have learned, discussed, and resolved throughout this book. In this section, we will consider how our liturgical celebrations serve to turn people's hearts to Christ.

Notice that this section is titled "engaging people in the liturgy," not "creating an engaging liturgy." The distinction may seem minor, but it is much more profound than the inclusion or omission of a few words might initially indicate. What we will consider here is not manipulating the celebration of the Eucharist or our sacramental life to somehow be or become something we are not. Our liturgical life is simply too important for such tactics. Rather, our focus will be giving the liturgy the attention and care it needs in order to help people to fully enter into the celebration, in such a manner that they may be led to act on their growing sense of belonging with Christ and with one another, or to encounter Christ more deeply than they have previously known. Leading people to be engaged with the liturgy is a critical goal for our attention.

We who bear responsibility for preparing or for ministering within the liturgy recognize that there are many pastoral and liturgical judgments that contribute to helping people fully enter into our liturgical prayer, or potentially prevent them from doing so. Ultimately, our desire must be to enact the liturgy in a manner that invites people into the mystery of God's love, united with Christ, whose very life and love we celebrate, through the power and urging of the Holy Spirit.

Engaging people in the liturgy requires us to prepare and to celebrate the liturgy with care, and to prepare people for the liturgy with the awareness that doing so offers a bridge between Christ's saving and sacrificial love and the ordinary yet profound nature of our human life. Put more simply, people's lives are often messy, chaotic, and confusing; none of us comes to the Eucharist with a completely pure heart; all of us need God's grace. And as we have seen, most people come to Mass week after week without being touched by the depth of all we express in the celebration of the Eucharist. The majority of people who come are not engaged, especially at Christmas, Easter, weddings, funerals, baptisms, or celebrations of First Holy Communion. At these moments, an overwhelming number of people present are likely to be not engaged or are actively disengaged. It is likely that taking this into consideration when we prepare and celebrate the liturgy will challenge us to look at small things that can make a big difference in the way we pray together. This also helps to highlight the benefit of engaging people through faith formation and community-building connected to these liturgical and sacramental celebrations.

Of course, there is not one simple way in which to engage people in our liturgical prayer. There are, however, consistent elements of liturgical preparation and catechesis that we can explore in light of all we have learned and discussed throughout the reading of this book. What follows is not intended to be exhaustive; whole volumes have been written about each of the elements explored here. Rather, the list below is a simple beginning point for conversation, exploration, evaluation, and preparation. You may consider discussing this within your spiritual life or worship committee, your pastoral council, or in a Two by Two process through which you hear the perceptions and hopes of the people of your community. Just as the celebration of the liturgy is too important for manipulation, it is also too important to be taken lightly, enacted in a manner that speaks of fulfilling obligations rather than with an appreciation of the responsibility of mediating Christ's saving love in action, word, sound, and silence. Engaging people in the liturgy is of greatest importance, and therefore worthy of our greatest attention and care.

Prior to the Liturgy: Hospitality

When people come to Sunday Mass at your parish, how are they greeted? Are those who seem confused or uncomfortable likely to meet someone who will show Christ's love through his or her actions or greeting? On occasions when there are many visitors, such as funerals or weddings, is there a worship aid that helps people understand our ritual actions and how to participate well?

As We Begin: Invitation to Prayer

As the celebration begins, is there any gesture or brief comment that invites people's full consciousness and prayer? Are people encouraged to offer their minds, hearts, and voices together as one body?

Proclamation

Is it clear that Christ is present through the proclamation of the Liturgy of the Word, through careful preparation, and through the ministry of lectors, who are representative of the whole community?

Music

Is music selected and performed in ways that invite the people's participation? Are the cantors or choir mindful of their role of enabling the sung prayer of the assembly?

Homily

Does the homily offer people real-life examples of gospel living? In what ways are people drawn into the call and challenge of Christ through the homily? Are there questions for reflection and sharing in the Sunday bulletin, on the parish website, or used at parish meetings throughout the week?

Pacing

Do people have the sense that the liturgy is rushed? Or, are there awkward pauses in which the liturgical action seems confused or lost?

Silence

Is the need for sacred silence acknowledged and marked during the celebration?

Sending

How are people given the sense that their encounter with Christ in the Eucharist is to be carried out in mission throughout the coming week?

Before and After: Liturgical Catechesis

How are people helped to understand our liturgical actions, feasts, and seasons? How are they encouraged to prepare their hearts and minds for the celebration of the liturgy and to reflect upon it after the celebration? Is there a regular rhythm of liturgical catechesis with children, youth, adults, and families?

Engaging Youth for a Lifetime of Faith

M uch has been written and discussed in the last ten years about evangelizing youth in a manner that will nurture and sustain lasting faith in the next generation of Catholic Christians. Particularly since the publication of the National Study of Youth and Religion,[43] and heightened by the Pew Forum study that indicates that most of the people who leave the church of their childhood do so before age 24, engaging youth and younger adults is a true desire and dilemma for pastoral leaders. Like the brief postscript on the liturgy, this final section on engaging youth is not intended to be an exhaustive treatment of youth ministry principles, or processes. Rather, this is a brief exploration of what we have learned, discussed, and explored together in this book, applied to our ministry to and with youth and younger adults, engaging them for a lifetime of faith.

First, a few brief observations about the developmental needs of youth: As children mature, their world increasingly becomes more complex, filled with greater social interaction, development of talents, skills and interests, and a growing desire for independence. Youth grow in their appreciation of ambiguity, abstract concepts, and the mysteries of life, love, and faith. Their desire for a better world is often inspiring, as is their willingness to actively serve in order to improve life for those who are in grave need of attention, care, food, clothing, shelter, and love.

Adults often misperceive the peer social interactions of adolescents as a world in which adults do not belong—yet most of us recall key relationships with adults during our teen years, often with parents and grandparents, sometimes with other adults with whom we enjoyed a special relationship. Christian Smith's summary report of the National Study on Youth and Religion echoes this important realization: "Contrary to popular misguided cultural stereotypes and frequent parental misperceptions, we believe that the evidence clearly shows that the single most important social influence on the religious and spiritual lives of adolescents is their parents."[44] The realization that youth themselves identify an appreciation for their parents' contribution to their spiritual development has led to critical conversations among pastoral leaders about the ways in which we may reach parents and other adults of influence in the lives of teens. From the perspective of our current discussions, we must make note that engaged adults will pass on our faith in compelling and convincing ways; building engagement within the community of faith will lead us to engage youth and younger adults for a lifetime of faith.

Taking all of our previous discussions to heart, we can begin to imagine a community in which youth have adult mentors, guides, and companions in their parents, grandparents, extended family, and through other willing adults in the community. In such a community, youth, like people of every age, know that they belong, are valued, and have a meaningful contribution to make.

✧ Include Youth in Your Discussions ✧

The process of engaging youth will be much like engaging people of any age, and will be most effectively accomplished by drawing young people into critical conversations about the role of the community in their lives and in the life of their peers. Invite a few young people to read and discuss this book with a group of interested adults. Study and discuss the essays and videos that are the result of the National Symposium on Adolescent Catechesis at www.niac.org. Later, create Two by Two teams of an adult and a young person to actively listen to other young people in your parish.

Consider these broad elements for your conversation and evaluation:

Meeting Spiritual Needs

Are the spiritual needs of your youth and younger adults met through liturgies that are celebrated with passion and a sense of reverence and awe in Christ's presence? Are young people likely to meet and encounter others with a real desire to follow Christ with their lives?

Meaningful Service

Do young people have the opportunity to offer themselves in meaningful ways in your parish? Are youth and younger adults regularly acknowledged for the contributions they make to life within your parish and to those in need in your local community and in the world?

Belonging

Are the younger members of your community truly valued, or is your parish one in which only those of a certain age or tenure in the parish seem to belong, with everyone else simply being tolerated?

Learning and Growing Together

Do youth have the opportunity to learn and grow in their peer groups and with adults in your parish? Do the younger members of your community have trusted adults with whom they can share their hopes and dreams, fears and spiritual needs?

Resources for Further Development

Pastoral leaders are busy people! Those who are parishioner leaders have work and family commitments; staff members balance multiple areas of responsibility; everyone has a limited amount of time to give to any initiative or plan. The resources that are listed here will make it possible for you to act on what you have discussed and planned in *Turning Hearts to Christ*. They have been developed with you in mind, to make it realistic for you to commit to engaging people in a lifetime of faith through the vision and strategies presented in this book.

A Free *Turning Hearts to Christ* Workbook: This free reproducible e-resource includes planning process worksheets and plan template, a Catholic study guide for Growing an Engaged Church, current parish practice tracking sheets, and samples of the resources listed below. Download this free workbook at www.thegenerousheart.com.

Many Points of Contact: This reproducible e-resource will equip you to incorporate Seasonal Renewal into the life of your parish. It includes outlines for a youth and adult pre-season meeting in which people prepare for the season to come, flyers to be distributed to parishioners to guide their conversation and reflection, and additional materials that are specific to the seasons. Many Points of Contact supports the seasons of renewal during Autumn Leading into Advent; Winter Leading into Lent; Annual Renewal of Discipleship and Stewardship; and Worship and Liturgy. A link for Many Points of Contact may be found at www.thegenerousheart.com and at www.pastoralplanning.com.

The Two by Two Project: This resource guides pastoral leaders through an active listening process that will facilitate your gathering of essential parishioner input for your parish's life. Companion Two by Two resources for Liturgy, Catechesis, Youth, and Stewardship are also available.

Living Your Strengths Pastoral Leader's Resource Kit and Small Group Process: While we have not dwelt on ways to help people identify, develop, and offer their God-given talents, this is crucial to your future efforts to build engagement. Living Your Strengths is a research-based talent identification process used in a growing number of dioceses and parishes. These resources have been developed to aid pastoral leaders in the early stages of talent-identification and strengths development, and can be found at www.thegenerousheart.com.

Additional samples, articles, and an email link to Leisa Anslinger are found at: www.thegenerousheart.com. Through this website readers may also connect with pastoral leaders who are already building engagement and fostering strengths development in their dioceses and parishes.

⌐ Bibliography ⌐

Winseman, Albert L. *Growing an Engaged Church* (New York: Gallup Press, 2007).

Cooperrider, David L. and Diana Whitney. *Appreciative Inquiry: A Positive Revolution in Change* (San Francisco: Barrett-Koehler Publishers, Inc., 2005).

Huebsch, Bill, with Leisa Anslinger. *Great Expectations: A Pastoral Guide for Partnering with Parents* (New London, CT: Twenty-Third Publications, 2010).

⌐ Endnotes ⌐

1 The U.S. Religious Landscape Survey, The Pew Forum on Religion and Public Life, 2008, http://religions.pewforum.org/reports.

2 http://cara.georgetown.edu/bulletin/index.htm#faq.

3 Pew Forum on Religion and Public Life, 2010.

4 Winseman, Albert L., *Growing an Engaged Church* (New York: Gallup Press, 2007).

5 See, for examples, the websites of St. Gerard Majella Parish (www.stgm-ajella.org), St. Matthew Parish (www.stmatthewcatholic.org), and St. Clare Parish (www.saintclareparish.org).

6 United States Conference of Catholic Bishops, *Go and Make Disciples*, tenth anniversary edition, 2002, 24-25.

7 United States Conference of Catholic Bishops, *National Directory for Catechesis*, 2005, 29C.

8 The steps detailed in this paragraph are an adaptation of Appreciative Inquiry. See endnote below for citation information.

9 Anslinger, Leisa and Victoria Shepp, *Forming Generous Hearts: Stewardship Planning for Lifelong Faith Formation* (New London, CT: Twenty-Third Publications, 2007).

10 Cooperrider, David L. and Diana Whitney, *Appreciative Inquiry: A*

Positive Revolution in Change (San Francisco: Barrett-Koehler Publishers, Inc., 2005).

11 See, for example, the Pew Forum Religious Landscape report: http://religions.pewforum.org/reports.

12 Winseman, Albert L., *Growing an Engaged Church*, 73-78.

13 Pope John Paul II, in *Novo Millennio Ineunte*, #43.

14 *Growing an Engaged Church*, 44.

15 *Growing an Engaged Church*, 83.

16 The Pew Forum on Religion and Public Life, *Faith in Flux: Changes in Religious Affiliation*, April 27, 2009.

17 "Pope announces formation of pontifical council for new evangelization," CNS, July 2, 2010.

18 Pope Benedict XVI, *Charity in Truth*, 5.

19 Ibid., 34.

20 *Go and Make Disciples*, 16.

21 *Growing an Engaged Church*, 67.

22 *Growing an Engaged Church*, 132.

23 *Growing an Engaged Church*, 40.

24 United States Conference of Catholic Bishops, *Our Hearts Were Burning Within Us*, 17.

25 United States Conference of Catholic Bishops, *Stewardship: A Disciple's Response*, tenth anniversary edition, 35.

26 Catherine Cronin Carotta and Michael Carotta, *Sustaining the Spirit* (New London, CT: Twenty-Third Publications, 2005), 32.

27 *Stewardship: A Disciple's Response*, 14.

28 *Gaudium et Spes*, 31.

29 *Stewardship: A Disciple's Response*, Introduction.

30 *Stewardship: A Disciple's Response*, 39.

31 *Stewardship: A Disciple's Response*, 19.

32 *Stewardship: A Disciple's Response*, Introduction.

33 *Go and Make Disciples*, 13.

34 *Go and Make Disciples*, 13.

35 *Stewardship: A Disciple's Response*, 14.

36 *Growing an Engaged Church*, 137.

37 *Growing an Engaged Church*, 107.

38 *National Directory for Catechesis*, 61A.7.

39 "Small communities bear big gifts," *National Catholic Reporter*, May 28, 1999.

40 *Growing an Engaged Church*, 70.

41 *Go and Make Disciples*, 16.

42 For a fascinating look at this perception which science bears out, see the Pace of Life study at: http://www.paceoflife.co.uk/.

43 See Smith, Christian, *Soul Searching: The Religious and Spiritual Lives of American Teenagers* (Oxford University Press, 2005); also www.niac.org, the website for the National Initiative on Adolescent Catechesis, for thorough and compelling essays and transcripts and videos from the National Symposium on Adolescent Catechesis.

44 *Soul Searching*, 261.

Forming Generous Hearts
Stewardship Planning for Lifelong Faith Formation
LEISA ANSLINGER and VICTORIA SHEPP

Conversion, discipleship, stewardship. The authors believe that these three giants of parish life are essential components of a vibrant parish. They provide indispensable principles to guide pastoral leaders as they seek to transform their parishes into places where people embrace and live Christian discipleship.

144 pages • $14.95 • order 956425 • 978-1-58595-642-5

Dreams and Visions
Pastoral Planning for Lifelong Faith Formation
BILL HUEBSCH

Here Bill urges parish leaders and ministers to move in the direction of lifelong faith formation by offering parishioners powerful conversion experiences. He also offers a clear and consistent plan for step-by-step growth, with special emphasis on excellent liturgies, strong and effective catechist and teacher formation, and developing households of faith.

144 pages • $14.95 • order 956388 • 978-1-58595-638-8

22 Steps to a Great Catholic Parish
Practical and Doable Ways to Improve Parish Life
JAMES N. REINHARDT

Here the author shares personal experiences and stories about how the parish can be the place where parishioners enthusiastically share and live their faith. Each of the twenty-two steps takes a parish closer to being not just good but great.

272 pages • $19.95 • order 957958 • 978-1-58595-795-8

1-800-321-0411 • WWW.23RDPUBLICATIONS.COM